GW00715796

KitchenAid

FOR EVERYTHING YOU WANT TO MAKE

HISTORY OF THE BRAND

A LEGEND IS BORN

INVENTION OF THE FIRST STAND MIXER AND BIRTH OF THE BRAND

1919

Nearly a century ago, Herbert Johnson, an engineer from Ohio, invented an extraordinary machine that would revolutionize the lives of professional cooks and aficionados alike: the H5, the first domestic electric mixer. While trying it out, the wife of one of the company managers unwittingly gave the brand its name when she exclaimed in delight, "I don't care what you call it, it's the best kitchen aid I've ever had." And KitchenAid was born. Over the years, the brand has never ceased to invent and innovate for food lovers, creating solutions inspired by the professional world.

THE STAND MIXER OF THE STARS

1927

GROWING POPULARITY AND RECORD SALES

The model that came after the H5 was an instant success; 20,000 units were sold in the three years immediately following its launch. Celebrities were the first to recognize the excellence of the KitchenAid stand mixer and put it to use, notably John Barrymore, Marion Davies, E.I. DuPont, Henry Ford, Myrna Loy, Fredric March, Ginger Rogers, and the governor of New York, Al Smith.

THE DESIGNER

THE SUCCESSFUL PAIRING OF STYLE AND CUTTING-EDGE TECHNOLOGY

Egmont Arens was a world-renowned designer who shared his talent with KitchenAid for a number of years. He designed three of the brand's most elegant models, including the famous Model K, now a modern classic. His highly acclaimed creations received many design awards and are found on display at many museums. More than 60 years later, KitchenAid mixers still look very much like the ones he designed, proof of his remarkable and visionary talent.

1936

TIMELESS DESIGN

...THAT HAS NEVER CHANGED

The K5A made its debut on the eve of WWII, and all three mixers designed by Egmont Arens remain practically unchanged to this day. They are exhibited as part of museum collections the world over, and they have won a number of major awards for their breathtaking design.

1941

A WORLD OF COLORS

Bright colors have become a hallmark of KitchenAid.

TASTES AND COLORS...

In 1955, in a world of kitchen appliances that was entirely white, the stand mixer was dressed in the brightest colors: rose petal pink, sunny yellow, island green, satin chrome, and old-fashioned copper. In 1994, the color palette grew and developed to suit the newest models: Empire Red, Cobalt Blue, Green Apple, Majestic Yellow, Metallic Charcoal, and even Tangerine, to the great delight of design connoisseurs.

1994

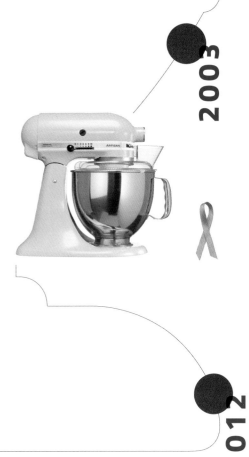

2003

KITCHENAID GETS ACTIVE

WOMEN'S CAUSES

All-around activism: KitchenAid's Cook for the Cure Program began working with the Susan G. Komen foundation to advocate for and support women in the fight against breast cancer. In honor of this new partnership, KitchenAid launched a limited-edition pink collection, with part of the profits donated to the foundation.

2012

A HELPING HAND

POWER AT YOUR FINGERTIPS
QUANTITY AND QUALITY

KitchenAid presented its new 6.9-liter bowl-lift stand mixer, the strongest, most powerful, quietest, and simply the best stand mixer in its category. Its 1.3-horsepower motor allows it to mix large quantities quickly and efficiently in its 6.9-liter stainless steel bowl, guaranteeing exceptional performance. This model took the 2012 Küchen Innovation prize for its quality, functionality, and design. Once again, KitchenAid would hold its place at the cutting edge of innovation and excellence in the twenty-first century.

A COMPLETE RANGE OF KITCHEN APPLIANCES, FROM BIG TO SMALL

FROM STORAGE TO PREPARATION, FROM PREPARATION TO COOKING

KitchenAid launched its new line of Vertigo refrigerators and wine cellars, elegant household appliances that guarantee excellent storage conditions and can be installed in any kitchen. This launch also included the Artisan line of kitchen appliances: the 4-liter stand mixer, electric kettle, hand blender, 2-slice and 4-slice toaster, and 2.1-liter and 3.1-liter stand mixers.

2013

2015

A REVOLUTIONARY LAUNCH

A YEAR OF MAJOR CHANGES

There was a revolution in the culinary world when KitchenAid launched its Artisan Cook Processor. Designed with creativity and simplicity in mind, this new appliance takes care of all the steps involved in making a dish, including chopping, mixing, and cooking.

2018

THE WORLD'S #1 MIXER BRAND

* (Source: Euromonitor International Limited; Consumer Appliances 2018 edition, retail volume sales, 2012 – 2017 Mixer Category data (includes stand mixers & hand mixers).®/TM ©2017 KitchenAid. All rights reserved.)

FIND YOUR MIXER MATCH

1. PICK A SIZE

3.3 L
Master of the dinner for two? Opt for the "Mini" version, ideal for small-scale cooking.

4.8 L
The classic standard mixer, perfect for 4 to 6 people. A wedding registry essential!

6.9 L
Are you a master baker or someone with a big family to feed? Choose our Bowl Lift model, inspired by professional design and applications.

2. PICK A COLOR

Choose the color that matches your personality.

3.3 L	4.8 L		6.9 L
● Hot Sauce	○ White	● Candy Apple	● Empire Red
● Matte Black	○ Café Latte	● Almond Cream	● Onyx Black
● Matte Grey	● Majestic Yellow	○ Silk Pink	● Candy Apple
● Guava Glaze	● Tangerine	● Raspberry Ice	○ Frosted Pearl
● Honeydew	● Espresso	● Cranberry	● Medallion Silver
● Twilight Blue	○ Frosted Pearl	● Pistachio	
	● Medallion Silver	● Green Apple	
	● Glacier Blue	● Chrome	
	● Crystal Blue	● Brushed Nickel	
	● Blueberry	● Copper	
	● Plumberry	● Onyx Black	
	● Boysenberry	● Contour Silver	
	● Empire Red		

3. CHOOSE YOUR ACCESSORIES

FOR CULINARY PREPARATIONS

 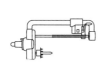

- Vegetable Sheet Cutter (see p. 16)
- Spiralizer with Peel, Core and Slice (see p. 17)
- Food Processor Attachment (see p. 18)
- Citrus Juicer (see p. 19)
- Sauce attachment (see p. 20)
- Fruit and Vegetable Strainer (see p. 21)
- Fresh Prep Slicer/Shredder (see p. 22)

FOR PASTA AND GRAINS

- Pasta Sheet Roller & Cutter Set (see p. 23)
- Ravioli Maker (see p. 24)
- Pasta Press (see p. 25)
- Pasta Drying Rack (see p. 23)
- Grain Mill (see p. 26)

FOR MEAT-BASED SAVORY DISHES

- Metal Food Grinder Attachment (see p. 27)
- Food Grinder (see p. 27)
- Sausage Stuffer (see p. 27)

FOR SWEET TREATS

- Ice Cream Maker (see p. 28)
- Sifter and Scale Attachment (see p. 29)

ATTACHMENT DESCRIPTIONS

WIRE WHIP

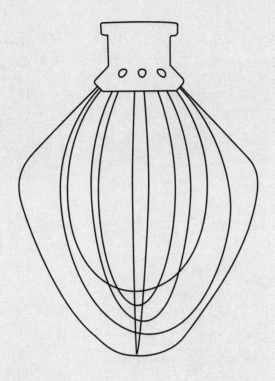

USE

Begin by whipping on the lowest speed setting, then gradually increase the speed. If you whip rapidly from the start, you risk incorporating less air into your mixes and creating a heavier result. You should also be careful to avoid using the wire whip to work cold butter mixes, because this may cause an unusable mass of dough to collect in the center of the whip.

DISHES

The wire whip will let you beat air into mixtures to make:
- Whipped egg whites
- Egg white meringues (see p. 42), etc.
- Savory or sweet mousses: Floating Islands (see p. 306)
- Mayonnaise (see p. 30)
- Whipped cream (see p. 43)
- Sweet dishes: Raspberry macarons (see p. 300), Amaretti (see p. 302), Waffles (see p. 88), Crepes with salted caramel (see p. 96), etc.
- Savory creations: Buckwheat galette millefeuille with crab (see p. 192), Cream of butternut squash (see p. 160)

D O U G H
H O O K

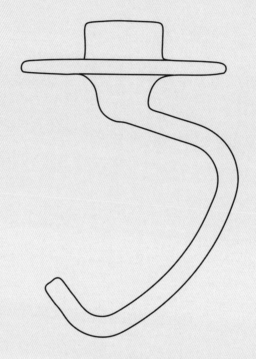

USE

Before attaching the dough hook to the mixer, mix all the dry ingredients in your recipe with the flat beater to evenly distribute them. Then use the dough hook as you gradually add the wet ingredients. Let the mixer run briefly to make a ball of dough. Continue kneading for a few minutes to make a smooth, elastic dough, which you can then let rise in the bowl.

DISHES

The dough hook is your best friend for superb dough-base creations, including:
- Breads: Gluten-free bread (see p. 218), Seed bread (see p. 68), Cheese naans (see p. 50), Classic "Nanterre" brioche (see p. 72), Viennese baguettes (see p. 80), etc.
- Kneaded pastries: Puff pastry (see p. 37), White pizza with ambercup squash, mushrooms, and walnuts (see p. 62)
- Bread-based snacks: Sweet (see p. 288) or savory pretzels, Breadsticks (see p. 52), Fougasse (see p. 60)

and fresh pasta, such as:
- Spaghetti (alla passata p. 230, carbonara p. 232)
- Tagliatelle (with pesto, p. 238)
- Cannelloni (see p. 228)
- Lasagne (see p. 234)

attachment
descriptions

FLAT BEATER

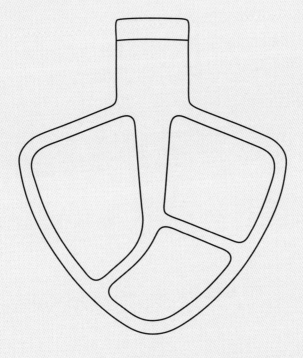

USE

Like the wire whip, start running the flat beater on the lowest setting, then gradually increase the speed to the desired level. This will help you avoid splatter and make uniform mixtures.

DISHES

The real jack-of-all-trades of your Artisan mixer, you can use the flat beater for any preparation that does not require the use of the wire whip or dough hook.
It is ideal for:
- Making snacks: Scones (for a raisin version, see p. 78), Pistachio éclairs (see p. 292), etc.
- Making cakes: Sun-dried tomato, olive, and feta cake (see p. 56), Chocolate fondant (see p. 94), etc.
- Mashing cooked vegetables: Mashed sweet potatoes with ham (see p. 190)
- Beating cold sauces
- Making flavored butters
- Making pastry for pies and tarts: Banana-caramel (banoffee) pie (see p. 256), Quiche Lorraine (see p. 64), Ricotta and pine nut tart (see p. 264), etc.
- Making choux pastry: Chouquettes (see p. 70), Cheese puffs (Gougères; see p. 48)

attachment
descriptions

FLEX EDGE BEATER

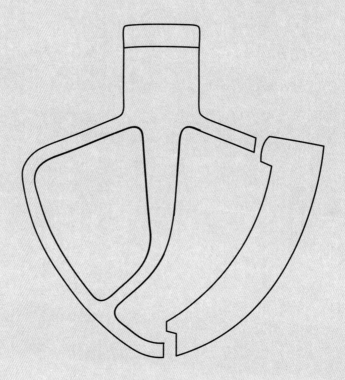

USE

The flex edge beater lets you mix together the ingredients in your preparation without having to stop the mixer or use a spatula. Its unique design smoothly scrapes down the sides of the bowl as it mixes, creating a perfect, quick, and effortless result.

DISHES

It is useful for making recipes such as:
- Cakes of all kinds: Raspberry and lemon cake (see p. 86), Pecan brownies (see p. 84), Banana bread (see p. 82), Chocolate peanut cookies (see p. 90)
- Savory and sweet tarts: Alsatian tarte flambée—Flammekueche (see p. 222), Apricot and pistachio cream tart (see p. 254), etc.
- Pasta: Pumpkin gnocchi with sage butter (see p. 250), etc.

attachment
descriptions

POURING SHIELD

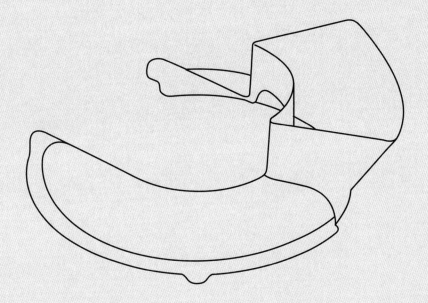

USE

The pouring shield is a practical two-in-one accessory that will let you avoid splatter while carefully adding ingredients with the mixer running; the funnel lets you add ingredients without directly pouring them onto the beater, dough hook, or wire whip. Made of transparent Lexan, it lets you see through to the ingredients already in the bowl.

VEGETABLE SHEET CUTTER

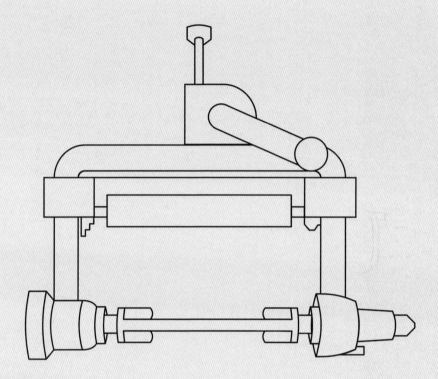

USE

Reinvent your favorite recipes with this attachment, which will let you cut neat sheets from a wide variety of fruits and vegetables. It peels, cuts, and cores with incredible ease, and its two blades let you make sheets of various thicknesses.

DISHES

Find simple, innovative ways to use fruit and vegetables to replace carbohydrates or avoid gluten on a daily basis in traditional recipes:
- Potato gratin with Roquefort cheese (see p. 204)
- Vegetable lasagne (see p. 236)

Or simply enjoy some gourmet dishes:
- Zucchini rolls with cod, bell peppers, and beurre blanc (see p. 140)
- Veggie rolls (see p. 116)
- Apple rose tart (see p. 258)

SPIRALIZER WITH PEEL, CORE AND SLICE

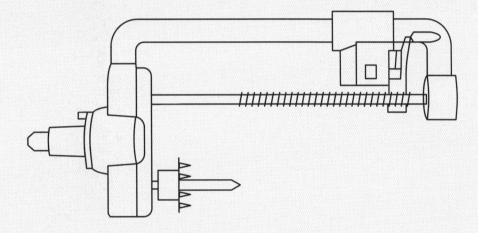

USE

With its three interchangeable blades, this attachment offers various slicing options:
- Coring fruit or vegetables while cutting them into fine ribbons
- Peeling fruit and vegetables while cutting them into fine ribbons
- Peeling fruit and vegetables

DISHES

It's ideal for gluten- or carbohydrate-free recipes, and when following a healthy, balanced diet, the spiralizer is an essential accessory for light, creative cooking. It lets you cut fruit and vegetables into neat, curly ribbons and make:
- Vegetable noodles with cream sauce and sun-dried tomatoes (see p. 130)
- Avocado toast (see p. 114)
- Curly fries with paprika (see p. 206)
- Asian tofu salad (see p. 138)

And also your own original creations!

FOOD PROCESSOR ATTACHMENT

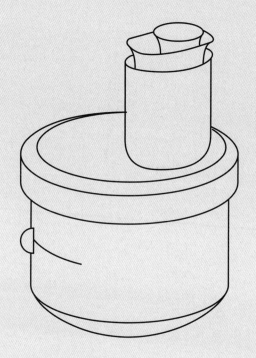

USE

This accessory creates considerable reductions in the preparation time of many recipes. It minces, shreds, slices, and juliennes foods quickly and precisely. Its exclusive ExactSlice™ system offers six different sizes, so you can make slices in the thickness of your choice. Control the thickness of the slices with an external manual lever, which ensures that all foods, firm and soft alike, are cut precisely and meticulously.

DISHES

- Potato and vegetable rosti (see p. 126)
- Guacamole (see p. 108)
- Salmon tartare (see p. 162)
- Zucchini, ricotta, and salmon (gluten-free) blinis (see p. 120)

attachment
descriptions

CITRUS JUICER

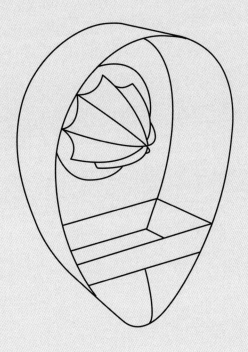

USE

The citrus juicer lets you squeeze the juice from large amounts of citrus fruit in no time while filtering out the pulp.

DISHES

- Orange and carrot salad with orange flower water (see p. 144)
- Scallop carpaccio with ginger and lime (see p. 196)

attachment
descriptions

SAUCE ATTACHMENT

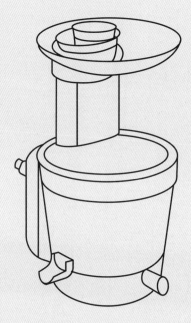

USE

Give yourself the perfect blend of taste and health with this accessory. Its two-stage slow juicing technology preserves the food's nutrients while reducing the amount of pulp and the time required. You can choose the pulp texture and density you want for your preparations using the three pulp screens: low pulp, high pulp, and sauce.

DISHES

These ingenious choices let you crush, grind, and puree an endless range of ingredients, such as fresh herbs, fruit, and vegetables, whether they be soft, firm, leafy, thin, or thick, etc. Give immediate life to all your culinary dreams, making dishes that include:
- Fresh fruit juices packed with vitamins: Antioxidant juice (see p. 106), Energy juice (see p. 100), Draining juice (see p. 104), Green juice (see p. 102)
- Essential cocktails: Piña colada (see p. 156), Strawberry daiquiri (see p. 154), Caribbean punch (see p. 152)
- Flavorful sauces to accompany your creations
- Mashed vegetables and creams
- Homemade jams and preserves

attachment
descriptions

FRUIT AND VEGETABLE STRAINER

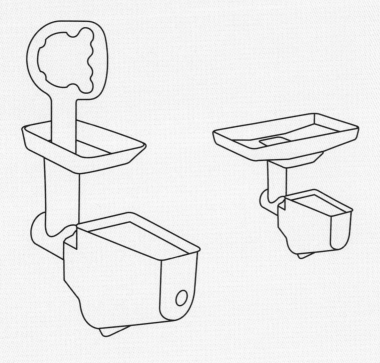

USE

The fruit and vegetable strainer is attached to the food grinder assembly. Place the ingredients in the feed tube and use the food pusher/wrench to guide them into the hopper. From the other end, collect a smooth mixture free from any seeds, stems, or skins.

DISHES

- Panna cotta (see p. 320)
- Cucumber gazpacho with spicy cream (see p. 112).

FOOD TRAY

USE

The food tray can be used in combination with the fruit and vegetable strainer (or food grinder, see p. 27); this ample tray lets you process ingredients in large quantities for quicker, easier work.

FRESH PREP SLICER/SHREDDER WITH SHREDDING AND GRATING ACCESSORY PACK

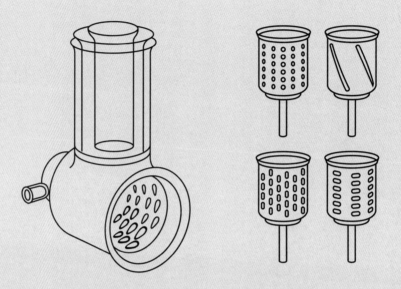

USE

The Fresh Prep slicer/shredder is particularly useful for easily cutting large and small fruit and vegetables into attractive, even pieces. It comes with a set of three interchangeable blades: two shredding blades (medium and coarse) and one slicing blade. It can slice, shred, mince, and chop various ingredients, such as nuts, blocks of chocolate (for example, for glazes), or even cheese. There are also three additional blades for the slicer/shredder: a julienne blade, a puree blade, and a fine shredding blade.

DISHES

- Tzatziki (see p. 110)
- Cheese soufflés (see p. 202)
- Ginger cake (see p. 272)

PASTA SHEET ROLLER AND CUTTER SET

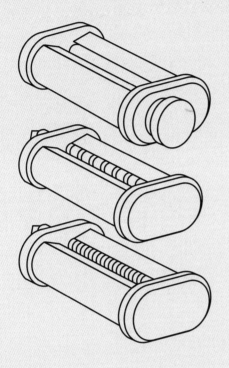

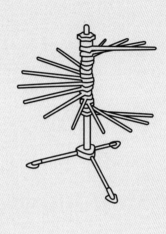

USE

This set, which includes the pasta sheet roller and two pasta cutters, is designed to let you easily make soft, thin pasta in any size you want. An initial run through the pasta sheet roller lets you make sheets of pasta in various thicknesses; you only need to select the desired thickness according to the type of pasta you want to make. Then use one of the cutters to make perfect spaghetti or tagliatelle.

DISHES

Lasagne, spaghetti, tagliatelle, linguine, etc. You can make any kind of traditional long pasta. Then take them to the next level with these simple recipes:

- Shrimp pad Thai (see p. 198)
- Spaghetti alla passata (see p. 230)
- Pesto tagliatelle (p. 238)

PASTA DRYING RACK

USE
Practical and compact, this tool lets you dry your pasta quickly and evenly without taking up your entire work surface.

RAVIOLI MAKER

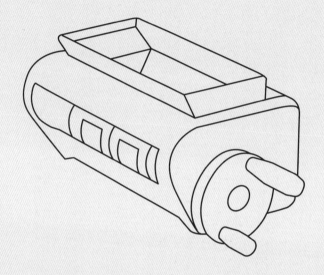

USE

As its name suggests, this is the essential accessory for making homemade ravioli without too much effort. Make a filling with the food grinder (see p. 27), roll out your fresh pasta, and let the ravioli maker do the rest. To make professional-looking ravioli, use with the pasta sheet roller (see p. 23); it will let you make thin, uniform sheets of pasta.

DISHES

The ravioli maker brings together filling and pasta with precision, stuffing three rows of ravioli before pinching and sealing the edges for perfectly uniform results. It's up to you to choose which dish you'd like to eat the most:

- Asian-style pork ravioli (see p. 224)
- Spinach and ricotta ravioli (see p. 226)

attachment
descriptions

PASTA PRESS

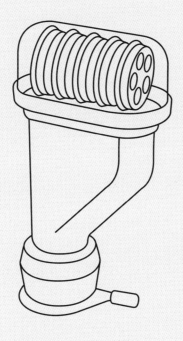

USE

With its intuitive design, this accessory is perfect for effortlessly making fresh pasta of any size and thickness in the shape of your choice. Just choose one of the six pasta discs, place the dough in the press, and turn on the mixer. Cut the pasta off when you're happy with their length.

DISHES

Make six different types of pasta, and serve them in an endless variety of ways:

- Spaghetti: Spaghetti carbonara (see p. 232)
- Bucatini: Bucatini all'amatriciana (see p. 240)
- Rigatoni: Cheese and pepper rigatoni (see p. 248)
- Fusilli: Fusilli alla burrata with shrimp (see p. 242)
- Mini macaroni: Mini macaroni and cheese (see p. 246)
- Large macaroni: Macaroni with porcini and thyme (see p. 244)

GRAIN MILL

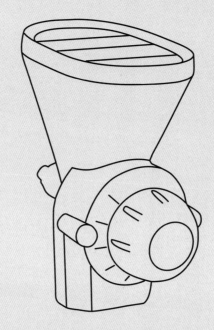

USE

The grain mill is practical for working with a variety of dry grains. It can also be used for dried beans or chickpeas. It can be set to mill your ingredients finely or crush them coarsely, according to the fineness that you want. Do not use the grain mill to grind coffee beans, oily nuts, or seeds; the oil they contain may damage the mechanism.

DISHES

The grain mill makes it easy to prepare:
- Flours: Rice flour (see p. 30)
- Breakfast creations: Corn muffins (see p. 212), Gourmet granola and almond milk (see p. 214), etc.
- Other dishes: Buddha bowl: Rice pilaf and vegetables (see p. 220)

attachment
descriptions

FOOD GRINDER

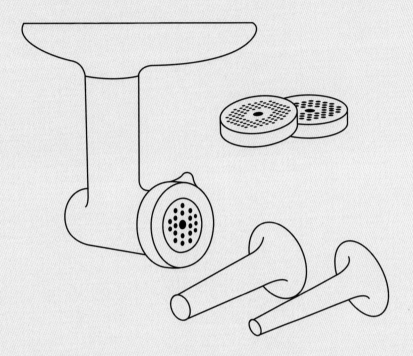

USE

This accessory—which comes in both metal and plastic versions—has a self-sharpening knife with four stainless steel blades, two stainless steel plates for coarse or fine chopping, and a combination food pusher-wrench.

DISHES

The food grinder's many uses make it an Artisan mixer essential. Its coarse and fine grinding plates let you slice, chop, and grind meat and fish; mill bread crumbs; crush nuts; and puree various foods. For example, you can make:
- Curried chicken balls (see p. 180)
- Country-style terrine (see p. 168)
- Chicken salad with lemongrass (see p. 186)
- Stuffed tomatoes (see p. 184)
- Stuffed Christmas turkey (see p. 188)

SAUSAGE STUFFER ACCESSORY

USE

This accessory is used in combination with the food grinder. It is equipped with two tubes (10 mm and 16 mm) to make sausages of different sizes.

DISHES

The sausage stuffer will let you effortlessly make delicious homemade sausages from the fresh meats of your choice or vegetarian sausages:
- Chorizo (see p. 174)
- Sausages with herbs (see p. 176)

ICE CREAM MAKER

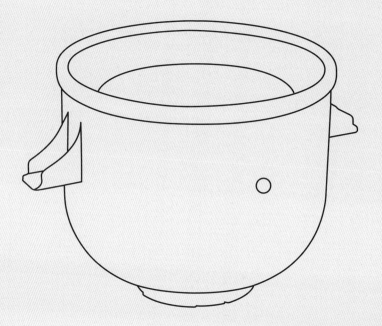

USE

With this ice cream maker, you can make up to 1.9 liters of ice cream or sorbet in less than half an hour. The liquid contained between the double walls of the ice cream mixer bowl ensures complete freezing throughout the churning process. Don't forget to put the bowl of the ice cream maker in the freezer the night before; this will chill the bowl thoroughly and help your creation to freeze more quickly.

DISHES

Creamy ice cream, refreshing sorbet, frozen desserts of all types, and tastier every day—the possibilities are endless, so let your imagination run wild! Here are a few examples to get you started:
- Lemon sorbet (see p. 148)
- Almond milk apricot ice cream (see p. 312)
- Caramel ice cream (see p. 314)
- Frozen yogurt (see p. 316)
- Cookie ice cream (see p. 308)

SIFTER AND SCALE ATTACHMENT

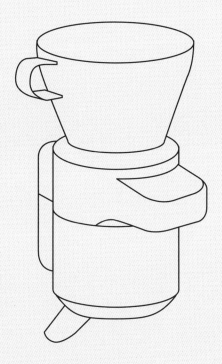

USE

The sifter and scale attachment is the essential accessory for making flawless creations. With its digital scale, which precisely weighs out the required ingredients, it removes any and all lumps and impurities from flour, sugar, and other dry ingredients, sifting them directly into the bowl of the mixer as it runs. It's a quick, effective way to make all kinds of light, fluffy recipes.

DISHES

With the sifter, you can make perfect, light versions of all your favorite bakery creations:
- Dacquoise (see p. 280)
- French strawberry cake (see p. 276)
- Macarons (see p. 300)

RICE
FLOUR

01. Pour the tapioca and rice into the grain mill set to the finest setting and run the mixer on speed 10.

Makes 450 g flour

Preparation time: 5 minutes

225 g tapioca

225 g white basmati rice

MAYONNAISE

01. Put the egg yolk, vinegar, mustard, salt, and pepper into the bowl of the mixer fitted with the wire whip.

02. Start the robot on speed 4 and beat for 1 minute.

03. When well combined, raise the speed to 8 and gradually pour in the oil in a fine stream.

Serves 4

Preparation time: 5 minutes

1 egg yolk

1 tbsp vinegar

1 tsp mustard

150 g neutral oil

Salt

Pepper

PASSATA

Serves 4

Preparation time: 10 minutes

Cooking time: 10-15 minutes

1 kg tomatoes

2 tbsp olive oil

Salt

01. Wash the tomatoes, cut them in half, and remove their seeds. Discard the excess liquid. Chop coarsely.

02. Cook in a frying pan with the olive oil for 10-15 minutes; they should begin to break down.

03. Season with salt, then puree into a coulis using the fruit and vegetable strainer on speed 4.

● TIP

Make large quantities of this sauce during the summer when tomatoes are good-quality and cheap. Sterilize and store in jars.

03

PESTO

Serves 4

Preparation time: 5 minutes

50 g basil

2 cloves garlic

50 g pine nuts

50 g Parmesan cheese

80 ml olive oil

Salt

01. Wash the basil and peel the garlic. Toast the pine nuts in a dry frying pan for 5 minutes, stirring constantly.

02. Place the basil (stems and leaves), garlic cloves, and pine nuts into the sauce attachment on speed 4.

03. Transfer the mixture to the bowl of the mixer fitted with the wire whip, grate in the Parmesan cheese using a cheese grater, and with the mixer running on speed 4, gradually add the oil, and a pinch of salt.

● TIPS

Replace the basil with arugula (rocket) and the pine nuts with almonds.
You can also add a few dried tomatoes to make a red pesto.
To keep the pesto fresh, cover it with a thin layer of olive oil.

03

BURGER BUNS

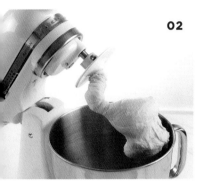

02

03

04

01. Pour 150 ml warm water into a bowl and add the yeast. Mix, then let stand for 5 minutes. Melt the butter.

02. In the bowl of the mixer fitted with the dough hook, mix the flour, salt, and sugar on speed 2. Next, add the softened yeast, milk, beaten eggs, and melted butter. Knead on speed 2 for 5 minutes. Let the dough rise for 40 minutes.

03. Turn the dough out onto a floured work surface, briefly knead by hand, then divide into 16 pieces of equal size. Form into balls and place on baking sheets lined with parchment (baking) paper. Let rise for 1 hour 30 minutes.

04. Preheat the oven to 180°C - 350°F (gas mark 4).
Brush the buns with the egg yolks mixed with a little water, then sprinkle with sesame seeds. Bake for 15-20 minutes. Cool on a wire rack.

Makes 16 buns

Preparation time: 10 minutes

Cooking time: 15–20 minutes

Resting time: 2 hours
10 minutes

810 g type-45 flour

13 g active dry yeast

55 g butter

13 g salt

40 g sugar

180 ml milk

3 eggs, beaten

2 egg yolks

100 g sesame seeds

FRESH PASTA

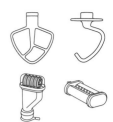

Serves 8

Preparation time: 10 minutes

Cooking time: 5 minutes

Resting time: 30 minutes

400 g type-45 flour

400 g semolina

8 eggs

1/2 tsp salt

01. Put the flour, semolina, and salt into the bowl of the mixer fitted with the flat beater. Mix on speed 2 and add the eggs. Mix until the dough begins to come together into a ball. Replace the flat beater with the dough hook. Knead the dough on speed 2 for 4 minutes. Sprinkle with flour, then refrigerate for 30 minutes.
Flour the dough again, then knead by hand for 1 minute.

02. If your recipe uses the pasta press: Divide it into small pieces, then run these through the gourmet pasta press fitted with the disc of your choice, consulting the user manual for the correct speed.

03-04. If your recipe uses the pasta sheet roller: Set the thickness to 1. On speed 2, make the dough more pliable by rolling it several times, folding it over between each roll. Next, turn the thickness to 2, then continue to reduce it incrementally to the desired thickness, making sure to flour the dough well to prevent it from sticking. Set on a floured towel.

05. Bring a large pot of salted water to a boil. Drop in the pasta and cook for about 5 minutes.

● **TIPS**

To make the pasta, the weight of the semolina-flour mix should be double that of the eggs; therefore, you should be sure to weigh them to obtain a good texture.
For pasta that is even firmer, you can increase the proportion of semolina to flour.
To vary the taste of your pasta, you can replace half of the type-45 flour with another flour: whole-wheat (wholemeal) flour or a whole-wheat mix, spelt flour, buckwheat flour, etc.

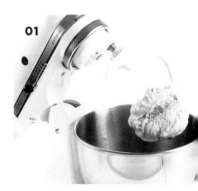

01

02

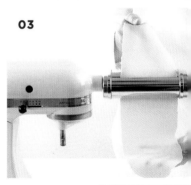

03

04

CHOUX PASTRY

01. Heat the water, milk, salt, and butter (cut into small cubes). As soon as the mixture boils, remove from heat and add all the flour at the same time.
Stir briskly until the dough forms a ball. The ball should be a little dry, so don't hesitate return the saucepan to the heat while you mix.

02. Place the ball of dough into the bowl of the mixer fitted with the flat beater. Start the mixer on speed 1, then add the eggs a little at a time, in four or five batches. Be careful toward the end; the dough should be supple, neither too dry nor too liquid. It should form a peak at the end of the flat beater.

Makes about 60 small cream puffs

Preparation time: 10 minutes

150 g water

100 g low-fat (semi-skimmed) milk

100 g unsalted butter

5 g salt

150 g type-45 flour

4 small eggs (about 240 g)

PIZZA DOUGH

01. Dissolve the fresh yeast in the warm water.

02. Mix the flour and salt in the bowl of the mixer. Attach the dough hook to the mixer. Add half of the water-yeast mixture, then start the mixer on speed 2 for 2 minutes.

03. Mix the oil with the remaining water-yeast mixture, then pour into the bowl and knead for another 4-5 minutes.

04. Cover the bowl and let rise for about 1 hour.

Makes dough for 5 pizzas

Preparation time: 5 minutes

Resting time: 1 hour

15 g fresh yeast

450 g warm water

750 g type-45 flour

15 g salt

7 1/2 tbsp olive oil (about 60 g)

SAVORY (SHORTCRUST) PASTRY

Serves 6-8 (one 20-cm pie plate or cake ring)

Preparation time: 10 minutes

Resting time: 30 minutes

200 g type-55 flour

100 g unsalted butter

2 g salt

35 g warm water

01. Put the flour, salt, and butter (cut into cubes) into the bowl of the mixer fitted with the flat beater. Mix on speed 2 for about 2 minutes.

02. Once the mixture has a sandy texture, replace the flat beater with the dough hook. Gradually add the water while kneading on speed 2.

03. Once the dough is smooth, use your hands to shape it into a ball, wrap in plastic wrap (clingfilm), and refrigerate for at least 30 minutes.

SWEET PASTRY

03

01. Put the softened butter into the bowl of the mixer fitted with the flex edge beater and mix on speed 4 for 3 minutes.

02. Add the confectioner's (icing) sugar and the salt, then mix on speed 4 for 2 minutes. With the mixer still running, add the egg. Lastly, on speed 2, add the flour and almond meal (ground almonds).

03. Form the dough into a ball and wrap in plastic wrap (clingfilm). Refrigerate for 1 hour.

04. Roll out the dough on a floured work surface and use to line a buttered, floured tart pan.

Makes 1 tart shell (case)

Preparation time: 10 minutes

Resting time: 1 hour

100 g butter

70 g confectioners' (icing) sugar

1 pinch salt

35 g eggs

175 g type-45 flour

30 g almond meal (ground almonds)

SHORTBREAD PASTRY

03

01. In the bowl of a mixer fitted with the flat beater, mix the flour, sugar, and salt on speed 1 for 30 seconds.

02. Cut the butter into cubes, add, and mix on speed 2 for 2 minutes. Finally, add the egg and mix until the dough just forms a ball.

03. Wrap the dough in plastic wrap (clingfilm) and refrigerate for 30 minutes.

Serves 8

Preparation time: 5 minutes

Resting time: 30 minutes

250 g type-45 flour

40 g superfine (caster) sugar

3 pinches salt

125 g butter

1 egg

PUFF PASTRY

Makes 1 tart shell (275 g pastry)

Preparation time: 45 minutes

Resting time: 2 hours

125 g flour

1/4 tsp salt

60 g water

90 g dry butter (84% fat content)

01. Pour the flour, salt, and water into the bowl of the mixer fitted with the dough hook. Knead on speed 2 for 5 minutes until it just comes together into a smooth dough.

02. Remove the bowl from the mixer, cover it with plastic wrap (clingfilm), and refrigerate for at least 30 minutes.

03. Meanwhile, soften the butter by pounding it with a rolling pin.
Roll the dough out into a long rectangle, place the butter in the middle, and fold the edges over the top.

04. Give the dough a quarter turn to the right, roll out into a long rectangle, and fold into thirds, letter style. Give it another quarter turn, again to the right. Roll out again into a long rectangle, then fold again into thirds, letter style.
Refrigerate the dough for 30 minutes. Repeat this process two times.
Once the puff pastry is ready, you can use it to make tart shells (cases), Napoleons, turnovers, etc.
It can also be frozen.

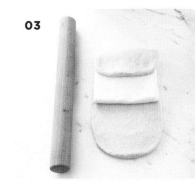

YEASTED PUFF PASTRY FOR CROISSANTS

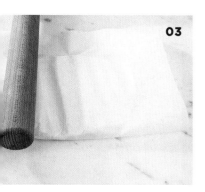

01. In the bowl of the mixer fitted with the dough hook, combine in the flour, salt, sugar, yeast, unsalted butter, egg, and milk.
Knead the mixture on speed 2 for 20 minutes, unsticking the dough with a rubber spatula or scraper, until the dough is just smooth.

02. Wrap the dough in plastic wrap (clingfilm) and refrigerate for at least 2 hours, preferably overnight.

03. Meanwhile, soften the butter by pounding it with a rolling pin.

04. At the end of the resting time, roll the dough out on a sheet of parchment (baking) paper into a long rectangle, place the butter in the middle, and fold the edges over the top.

05. Give the dough a quarter turn to the right, roll out into a long rectangle, bring the edges back into the center, fold in half, and give it another quarter turn, again to the right. Roll the dough out again into a long rectangle, then fold it into thirds, letter-style.
Refrigerate for 30 minutes.

Makes 48 pastries

Preparation time: 25 minutes

Resting time: 2 hours
30 minutes

750 g type-45 flour

15 g salt

75 g sugar

30 g compressed fresh yeast

75 g unsalted butter

1.5 egg

330 g milk

450 g dry butter (84% fat content)

basic
recipes

CLASSIC "NANTERRE" BRIOCHE

Makes 6 (25 x 10-cm) brioches

Preparation time: 25 minutes

Resting time: 1 hour 45 minutes

750 g fine wheat flour (or 690 g type-45 flour and 60 g wheat gluten)

75 g sugar

15 g salt

45 g fresh yeast

450 g eggs, cold

300 g butter (if possible, butter with 82% fat content)

01. Weigh the flour in the bowl of the mixer. Add the sugar and salt to one side of the bowl, then crumble in the fresh yeast on the other side of the bowl.

02. Add the cold eggs, then start the mixer fitted with the dough hook on speed 1. Knead for about 5 minutes.
Raise the speed to 2 and knead for another 5 minutes.
Lower the speed back to 1, then add the butter in two batches.
Once the butter is completely mixed in, raise the speed back to 2 and knead for about another 5 minutes, until the dough comes away from the sides of the bowl.

03. Let rest 45 minutes–1 hour at room temperature; this will give the dough time to develop its flavor.

04. Punch down the brioche dough by flattening it with the palm of your hand to release the gas from the yeast and let it rise again. Let the dough rest in the refrigerator for at least 30 minutes.

05. Cut the brioche dough into pieces of about 50 g each. Flatten each piece, then roll into balls between the palms of your hands. Let rest for 5 minutes. Repeat to make smooth balls, then refrigerate for 5 minutes.

02

04

05

ALMOND MILK

01. The previous day, soak the almonds in water for 12 hours.

02. The next day, drain the almonds and run them through the sauce attachment fitted with the fine pulp screen on speed 4, adding the mineral water. Keep in the refrigerator.

● TIPS

You can flavor the almond milk with vanilla extract or add a little agave syrup to sweeten it. You can also make non-dairy milks with other nuts: hazelnuts, cashews, etc. The leftover almond pulp that you can retrieve from the sauce attachment is called okara. You can run it through the mixer to refine its texture and use it to replace 30-40 g flour in the dough for tarts, cakes, cookies, etc. For example, it is delicious in cookies (see p. 90).

Makes 800 ml milk

Preparation time: 5 minutes

Resting time: Overnight

100 g almonds

800 ml mineral water

CHOCOLATE GANACHE

Serves 6

Preparation time: 5 minutes

Cooking time: 2 min

200 g dark chocolate

150 ml cream

20 g butter

01. Chop the chocolate with a knife and transfer to the bowl of the mixer.

02. In a saucepan, bring the cream to a boil. Pour over the chocolate and let stand for 2 minutes.

03. Mix with the flat beater on speed 2 for 3 minutes. When the mixture is completely blended, add the butter and mix for another 2 minutes. Use immediately or store in the refrigerator.

LEMON CURD

Serves 6-8

Preparation time: 10 minutes

Cooking time: 3 minutes

Resting time: 2 hours

120 g lemon juice

Zest of 1 lemon

110 g eggs

100 g superfine (caster) sugar

150 g butter

01. Put all the ingredients except the butter into a saucepan and bring to a boil, beating constantly. Cook for 3 minutes over medium heat, beating constantly, to thicken the mixture.

02. Transfer the mixture to the bowl of the mixer fitted with the wire whip, and with the mixer running on speed 8, add the butter in three batches.

03. Blend with an immersion (hand) blender. Refrigerate for at least 2 hours.

ITALIAN MERINGUE

01. Mix the water and sugar in a saucepan. Put the egg whites into the bowl of the mixer fitted with the wire whip.

02. Begin to heat the syrup. When it reaches 110°C, begin whipping the egg whites on speed 8. Heat the syrup until it reaches 121°C.

03. Turn down the mixer speed, then pour the syrup over the partially whipped egg whites a little at a time.

TURN the mixer speed back up and whip the meringue until it has cooled completely.

USE the meringue mixture to fill a pastry bag fitted with the tip of your choice.

Makes 450 g meringue

Preparation time: 20 minutes

60 g water

300 g superfine (caster) sugar

180 g egg whites

CUSTARD SAUCE (POURING CUSTARD)

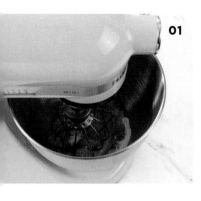

01. In the bowl of the mixer fitted with the wire whip, mix the egg yolks with the sugar on speed 4 for 3 minutes.

02. Meanwhile, heat the milk with the praline. Mix well to dissolve the praline. With the mixer running, gradually pour the boiling milk into the bowl of the mixer.

03. Pour the mixture back into the saucepan and cook over low heat, stirring constantly with a wooden spoon, until it begins to thicken. Once the cream coats the back of the spoon, remove the saucepan from the heat. Let cool, then keep in the refrigerator.

● **TIP**

Flavor the custard however you like: with pistachio paste, orange flower water, vanilla, cinnamon, or even chocolate. If you do not have any praline paste, replace it with homemade hazelnut spread (see p. 324).

Serves 4-6

Preparation time: 5 minutes

Cooking time: 5 minutes

6 egg yolks

100 g sugar

500 ml low-fat (semi-skimmed) milk

2 tsp praline paste

PASTRY CREAM

Makes 650 g pastry cream

Preparation time: 10 minutes

Cooking time: 5 minutes

Resting time: 1 hour

55 g superfine (caster) sugar

50 g cornstarch (cornflour)

100 g eggs (2 small eggs)

500 g low-fat (semi-skimmed) milk

1 vanilla bean (pod) or 1 tsp ground vanilla

1 pinch salt

1 knob of butter

01. Put 35 g sugar, the cornstarch (cornflour), and the eggs into the bowl of the mixer fitted with the wire whip. Start the mixer on speed 2, then gradually raise the speed to 6.

02. In a saucepan, heat the milk with 20 g sugar and the seeds from the vanilla bean until it just comes to a boil. Turn the mixer back on to speed 1, then gradually pour the boiling milk into the bowl. Whip for about 1 minute.

03. Return to the saucepan, then bring to a boil, whisking constantly. Let cook for another minute, still stirring. Remove from heat; add the salt and butter. Mix, then pour onto a plate and cover by laying a sheet of plastic wrap (clingfilm) directly onto the surface of the cream. Refrigerate for at least 1 hour.

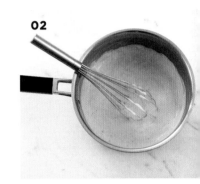

02

WHIPPED CREAM

Preparation time: 2 minutes

1 liter cream

01. Whip the cream, which should be cold, in the bowl of the mixer fitted with the wire whip on speed 8 for between 1 minute 30 seconds and 2 minutes.

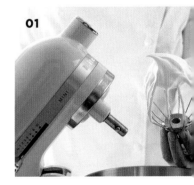

01

BASICS

BLINIS, SMOKED SALMON AND LEMONY CREAM

Serves 4–6

Preparation time: 20 minutes

Cooking time: 10 minutes

Resting time: 1 hour

BLINIS

250 ml milk

250 g type-45 flour

11 g active dry yeast

2 eggs

20 g butter

Salt

SALMON AND LEMONY CREAM

4 slices smoked salmon

200 ml whipping cream

1 tbsp mascarpone cheese

1 lemon

Chives

Salt

Freshly ground pepper

FOR THE BLINIS
Warm the milk. Combine the flour, salt, yeast, and warm milk in the bowl of the mixer with the flat beater and beat on speed 2 for 2 minutes. Use a spatula to scrape the batter out into a bowl. Let rest for 1 hour.

FOR THE LEMON CREAM
Whip the very cold whipping cream and the mascarpone in the bowl of the mixer fitted with the wire whip, gradually increasing the speed from 1 to 10 to make a Chantilly cream. Add the zest of the lemon and a drizzle of juice, a little finely chopped chives, a turn of the pepper mill, and a pinch of salt. Reserve in the refrigerator.

FINISHING THE BLINIS
Separate the egg whites from the yolks. Melt the butter. Using a spatula, fold the egg yolks and butter into the batter. Whip the egg whites to stiff peaks in the bowl of the mixer fitted with the wire whip, starting on speed 1 and gradually increasing to speed 8. Gently fold them into the batter.

Lightly oil a skillet or frying pan, then pour in small amounts of the batter, spacing them well apart. After a few minutes, check to see if the undersides are done and, if so, turn them over. When they are done, place them on a plate and repeat until you have used all the batter.

Serve the blinis warm with the salmon and cold lemony cream.

TIP

If you love the flavor of toasted dark wheat, substitute half of the flour with buckwheat flour.

CHEESE PUFFS (GOUGÈRES)

Makes about 60 small cheese puffs

Preparation time: 15 minutes

Cooking time: 25–30 minutes

Grate the cheese with a cheese grater.

FOR THE CHOUX PASTRY
Make the choux pastry as described on p. 34.

FOR THE TOPPING
Gently mix in the nutmeg, Espelette pepper, and 100 g of the grated Comté cheese. Fill a pastry (piping) bag fitted with a 13-mm plain tip (nozzle) with the pastry.

Preheat a convection (fan-assisted) oven to 160°C - 325°F (gas mark 3).
Pipe small mounds of the pastry about 2 cm in diameter onto nonstick baking sheets, spacing them well apart. Brush the cheese puffs with a beaten egg-yolk wash. Sprinkle with the remaining grated cheese and bake for 25–30 minutes.

CHOUX PASTRY

150 g water

100 g low-fat (semi-skimmed) milk

100 g butter, softened

5 g salt

150 g type-45 flour

4 large eggs (about 240 g)

TOPPING

140 g Comté cheese

1 pinch grated nutmeg

1 pinch Espelette pepper

1 egg yolk

VARIATION

You can sprinkle—or even add to the pastry—all kinds of seeds and nuts: poppy seeds, sesame seeds, chopped walnuts, or hazelnuts, etc.

CHEESE NAANS

Makes 4 naans

Preparation time: 30 minutes

Resting time: 1–2 hours

Cooking time: 15 minutes

340 g type-45 flour

2 g salt

2 g sugar

70 g warm water

10 g fresh yeast

15 g neutral oil

90 g plain (natural) yogurt

8 portions of The Laughing Cow® cheese

15 g butter

Put all the dry ingredients into the bowl of the mixer fitted with the dough hook. Add three-quarters of the warm water, the fresh yeast, oil, and yogurt. Turn on to speed 1 and knead for 10–15 minutes. Add the water as needed to achieve the right consistency; the dough should not be sticky.

Let rest in a bowl covered with a dish cloth for 1–2 hours. The dough should double or triple in volume.

Divide the dough into eight pieces, each weighing about 68 g. Shape into balls and use a rolling pin to flatten them to circles 18–20 cm in diameter.

Spread two portions of The Laughing Cow® cheese in the middle of four circles of dough, leaving a border of 1 cm all round. Brush this border with water. Top with the other four dough circles , pressing lightly to seal the edges.

Cook in a dry nonstick skillet or frying pan for 2–3 minutes on both sides or until the naans are done. Top with a few pats (knobs) of butter while they are still hot.

ALTERNATIVE

If you are not fond of cheese, you can make the naans with garlic and cilantro (coriander). In this case, chop 2 cloves of garlic and ¼ bunch of fresh cilantro. Brush the eight dough circles with a little olive oil and top with the chopped garlic and cilantro before cooking them in the skillet or frying pan.

BREAD-STICKS

Serves 4

Preparation time: 15 minutes

Cooking time: 20-25 minutes

Resting time: 30 minutes

200 g flour

30 g grated Mimolette cheese

6 g salt

5 g superfine (caster) sugar

5 g active dry yeast

100 ml warm water

40 ml olive oil

2 tbsp sesame seeds

2 tbsp poppy seeds

Put the flour, grated cheese, salt, sugar, yeast, water, and olive oil into the bowl of the mixer fitted with the dough hook. Knead on speed 2 for 10 minutes, just until the dough is smooth and elastic.
Turn the dough out onto a floured work surface, form it into a ball, cover with a cloth, and let rise for 30 minutes.

Preheat the oven to 200°C - 400°F (gas mark 6).
Cut the dough into many small pieces. Roll the pieces between your hands to make thin 10-cm ropes. Roll the ropes in the sesame and poppy seeds, then place them on a baking sheet lined with parchment (baking) paper. Bake for 20-25 minutes until golden brown.

TIPS

You may serve these breadsticks with tapenade. Substitute flaxseeds, spices (curry, caraway, etc.), or fresh herbs (thyme, rosemary, etc.) for the sesame and poppy seeds.

EGGS MIMOSA

6 eggs

Herbs (chives, parsley, etc.)

Salt

Pepper

MAYONNAISE

1 egg yolk

1 tbsp vinegar

1 tsp mustard

150 g neutral oil

Salt

Pepper

Hard-boil the eggs for 10–12 minutes in boiling water. Cool them immediately by placing them in cold water.

FOR THE MAYONNAISE
Make the mayonnaise as described on p. 30.

Peel the eggs and cut them in half lengthwise. Gently remove the yolks and press them through a fine mesh sieve. Mix them with 2 tablespoons of mayonnaise, then using a small spoon or a pastry (piping) bag fitted with a fluted tip (nozzle), put the mixture back into the halved whites.

GOT LEFTOVERS?

Make a sandwich with chopped eggs mimosa, a few chopped pickles and chives, and perhaps a crispy lettuce leaf. Add some mustard to the remaining mayonnaise, then mix it with some finely shredded celery root (celeriac) to make a remoulade.

SUN-DRIED TOMATO, OLIVE, AND FETA CAKE

Serves 4–6

Preparation time: 10 minutes

Cooking time: 45 minutes

150 g sun-dried tomatoes

4 eggs

200 g flour

11 g baking powder

100 ml white wine

50 ml olive oil

2 tbsp olives (green or black)

100 g feta cheese

3 pinches fleur de sel

Preheat the oven to 180°C - 350°F (gas mark 4).

In the bowl of the mixer fitted with the flat beater, mix the eggs, flour, baking powder, white wine, olive oil, and salt. Mix on speed 2 for 5 minutes. Add the sun-dried tomatoes, olives, and crumbled feta and mix on speed 2 for 1 minute.

Meanwhile, line a cake pan with parchment (baking) paper. Pour the batter into the pan and bake for about 45 minutes. If the cake begins to brown too much near the end of the baking time, reduce the temperature to 160°C - 325°F (gas mark 3). Let cool and serve.

VARIATIONS

You can replace the feta with another goat cheese or Emmental and substitute the sun-dried tomatoes with diced ham.

BAGELS
WITH CREAM CHEESE AND SALMON

Makes 8 (10-cm) bagels

Preparation time: 30 minutes

Cooking time: 40 minutes

Resting time: 40 minutes

60 ml warm water

22 g active dry yeast

375 g (preferably organic) white flour

3 tbsp superfine (caster) sugar

2 tsp extra fine salt (for bread making)

2 eggs

60 ml olive oil

Pumpkin seeds

300 g cream cheese

Pepper

Mesclun (salad mix)

Dill

8 slices smoked salmon

Mix the warm water and yeast in a bowl. Put the flour, sugar, salt, eggs, and oil in the bowl of the mixer fitted with the dough hook. Add the yeast-water mixture. Knead at speed 2 for 10 minutes until the dough forms a smooth ball, adding more flour if the dough is too sticky.

Transfer the dough ball to a bowl greased with 1 teaspoon of oil and turn to coat. Cover with a cloth and let rise for 30 minutes in a warm, draft-free place.

Once the dough has doubled in size, punch it down on a work surface. Make a ball, divide it into eight pieces, and roll each into a rope about 12 cm long. Bring the ends of each rope together and roll them together to seal. Place each ring on a baking sheet lined with parchment (baking) paper, cover with a cloth, and let rest for 10 minutes.

Preheat the oven to 200°C - 400°F (gas mark 6). Bring a pot water to a boil and drop in the bagels, cooking them for about 2 minutes and making sure to turn them over in the water. Let drain directly on the baking sheet and sprinkle with pumpkin seeds. Bake for 30 minutes.

Let the baked bagels cool on a rack, then slice in half.

Spread the bottom halves with cream cheese, then add pepper, a few leaves of mesclun (salad mix), and a little dill. Top with the smoked salmon and reassemble the bagels.

TIPS

These bagels can be frozen. You can sprinkle with a seed or spice mix or add lemon zest.

FOUGASSE

Serves 4

Preparation time: 20 minutes

Cooking time: 25 minutes

Resting time: 40 minutes

10 g active dry yeast

180 ml water

400 g flour

1 tbsp thyme

1 pinch salt

50 ml olive oil

10 pitted black olives

Combine the yeast and water in the bowl of the mixer fitted with the dough hook. Add the flour, olive oil, and salt. Knead on speed 2 for 20 minutes. Add the thyme and olives and knead for 1 minute, just enough to mix.

Cover the dough with a cloth and let rise in a hot place for 40 minutes.

Preheat the oven to 200°C - 400°F (gas mark 6).

Once the dough has risen substantially, place it on a baking sheet lined with parchment (baking) paper. Stretch it out and slash the top with a knife. Bake for about 25 minutes.

TIP

For a more gourmet fougasse, garnish with tapenade, pesto, bacon, cheese cubes, etc.

WHITE PIZZA WITH AMBERCUP SQUASH, MUSHROOMS, AND WALNUTS

Serves 4

Preparation time: 30 minutes

Cooking time: 20–25 minutes

Resting time: 1 hour

PIZZA DOUGH

3 g fresh yeast

90 g warm water

150 g type-45 flour

3 g salt

1 1/2 tbsp olive oil (about 12 g)

TOPPING

1/3 ambercup squash

4 button mushrooms

A drizzle of olive oil

50 g crème fraîche

A few walnuts, chopped

60 g grated Comté cheese

FOR THE PIZZA DOUGH
Make the dough as described on p. 34.

FOR THE TOPPING
Peel and cut the ambercup squash into slices about 4 mm thick.
Clean and finely slice the mushrooms. Quickly sauté them in a skillet or frying pan in a little olive oil so that they release their liquid.

Preheat the oven to 210°C - 410°F (gas mark 6).
Use a rolling pin to roll out the dough as finely as possible and in the shape that you prefer. Spread the crème fraîche over the entire surface of the dough. Top with the slices of ambercup squash, mushrooms, and chopped walnuts. Sprinkle with the grated Comté cheese.
Bake for 20–25 minutes.

FOR MEAT LOVERS

Coppa ham goes really well with this pizza! Arrange 4 slices on the pizza before sprinkling with the grated Comté cheese.

QUICHE LORRAINE

Serves 6–8 (20-cm pie dish or stainless-steel ring mold)

Preparation time: 20 minutes

Cooking time: 30-50 minutes

200 g smoked bacon

100 g Gruyère or Comté cheese

SAVORY (SHORTCRUST) PASTRY

200 g type-55 flour

100 g unsalted butter

2 g salt

35 g warm water

200 g smoked bacon

100 g Gruyère or Comté cheese

QUICHE FILLING

4 eggs

150 g crème fraîche

220 g low-fat (semi-skimmed) milk

1 tsp grated nutmeg

1 pinch Cayenne pepper

Salt

Pepper

FOR THE SAVORY (SHORTCRUST) PASTRY
Make the pastry as described on p. 35.

Cut the smoked bacon into fine slices. If you want to reduce the saltiness, blanch the slices in boiling water for 30 seconds. Sauté them quickly in a skillet or frying pan, but don't let them dry out. Drain to remove any excess fat.

FOR THE QUICHE FILLING
Put the eggs, crème fraîche, milk, and spices into the bowl of the mixer fitted with the wire whip. Whip on speed 2 for 1 minute, then on speed 4 for 1 minute.
Roll the dough to a thickness of about 3 mm and use to line a 20-cm diameter pie pan or stainless-steel ring mold. Prick the bottom of the dough with a fork and put it back into the refrigerator.

Preheat a convection (fan-assisted) oven to 180°C - 350°F (gas mark 4). Shred the cheese with the Fresh Prep slicer/shredder fitted with the medium shredding blade.
Arrange the bacon slices and cheese in the bottom of the quiche. Pour the quiche filling over them and bake for about 35 minutes.

VEGGIE VARIATIONS

For a meat-free quiche that still has a lovely smoky flavor, replace the bacon with smoked tofu or even smoked salmon.
For a lighter version, you can use a leek fondue instead of the bacon and cheese!

CHESTNUT BREAD

Serves 8

Preparation time: 10 minutes

Cooking time: 30 minutes

Resting time: 1 hour

600 g type-45 flour

100 g chestnut flour

600 ml warm water

20 g active dry yeast

2 tsp salt

Pour the warm water into the bowl of the mixer fitted with the dough hook and add the yeast. Knead on speed 1 for 2 minutes to dissolve the yeast.

Still on speed 1, gradually add the flours and salt, then knead on speed 2 for 6 minutes.

Flour your hands, then shape the dough into a ball and put it onto a baking sheet lined with parchment (baking) paper. Let rise for 1 hour in a warm place.

Preheat the oven to 210°C - 410°F (gas mark 6).
Use the tip of a knife to score a pretty pattern on the surface of the loaf and bake for 30 minutes. Let cool before slicing.

VARIATIONS

You can substitute the chestnut flour with rice flour, einkorn, whole wheat (wholemeal) flour or a whole-wheat mix. You can also add seeds and nuts.

SEED BREAD

Serves 6

Preparation time: 15 minutes

Cooking time: 40 minutes

Resting time: 2 hours
10 minutes

450 ml warm water

15 g active dry yeast

450 g type-65 flour

150 g rye flour

75 g type-80 flour

**150 g seed mix (pumpkin,
sunflower, poppy, etc.)**

7.5 g salt

Pour the warm water into the bowl of the mixer fitted with the dough hook and add the yeast. Knead on speed 1 for 30 seconds to dissolve the yeast. Add the flours, 75 g of the seed mix, and the salt; knead on speed 2 for 10 minutes. Form the dough into a ball, cover the bowl with a cloth, and let rise for 40 minutes in a warm place.

Once the dough has risen, punch it down with a spatula and knead by hand for 5 minutes. Form it into a ball, then place on a baking sheet lined with parchment (baking) paper. Sprinkle with the rest of the seed mix. Let rise for 1 hour 30 minutes in a warm place.

Preheat the oven to 200°C - 400°F (gas mark 6). Place a bowl of water on the lower oven rack to help the crust develop during baking. Bake for 25 minutes, then reduce the oven temperature to 180°C - 350°F and bake for another 15–20 minutes.

VARIATION

You can also use prepared multigrain flour mixes.

CHOUQUETTES

Makes about 60 small chouquettes

Preparation time: 15 minutes

Cooking time: 25–30 minutes

150 g water

250 g low-fat (semi-skimmed) milk

5 g salt

5 g sugar

100 g butter, softened

150 g type-45 flour

4 large eggs (about 240 g)

1 egg yolk

100 g nib (pearl) sugar

Make the choux pastry as described on p. 34.
Fill a pastry (piping) bag fitted with a 13-mm plain tip (nozzle) with the pastry.

Preheat the oven to 160°C - 325°F (gas mark 3).
Pipe small mounds of the dough about 2 cm in diameter onto nonstick baking sheets, spacing them well apart.
Brush the chouquettes with a beaten egg-yolk wash.
Sprinkle with nib (pearl) sugar.
Bake for 25–30 minutes.

VARIATIONS

You can also sprinkle them with cocoa nibs, brown sugar, crushed rose praline, etc. The possibilities are endless!
For a more gourmet version, cut each chouquette in half horizontally and fill with Chantilly cream.

TRADITIONAL "NANTERRE" BRIOCHE

Makes 2 25 x 10-cm brioches

Preparation time: 25 minutes

Cooking time: 18 minutes

Resting time: 3 hours
30 minutes

**225 g gluten-rich flour
(or 230 g type-45 flour
plus 20 g wheat gluten)**

25 g sugar

5 g salt

15 g fresh yeast

150 g cold eggs

**100 g butter (if possible,
82% fat content)**

1 egg

Make the brioche dough as described on p. 39.

Melt some butter and then brush the brioche molds with it. Divide the dough into two and place in the molds. Brush with beaten egg to glaze. Let rest in a warm place (for instance, in a turned-off oven with a bowl of hot water) at 25–30°C, and let rise for about 1 hour 45 minutes. Preheat a convection (fan-assisted) oven to 180°C - 350°F (gas mark 4).
Brush again with the beaten egg. Bake for about 18 minutes. Let cool on a rack.

VARIATION & ALTERNATIVE

You can add chocolate chips, raisins, chopped sugared almonds, etc. to the brioche dough. You can also flavor it with spices (saffron, cinnamon) or with grated citrus zest. If you cannot find fresh yeast, substitute it with 15 g of dry yeast dissolved in a little warm milk.

LEMON MADELEINES

Makes 12 madeleines

Preparation time: 15 minutes

Cooking time: 15 minutes

Resting time: 3–4 hours

70 g salted butter

85 g eggs

60 g sugar

5 g honey

20 g milk

Zest of 1 lemon

80 g type-55 flour

5 g baking powder

Heat the butter in a saucepan just until it browns. Remove from the heat and strain through a sieve.
Put the eggs, sugar, honey, milk, and lemon zest into the bowl of a mixer fitted with the wire whip. Beat for about 2 minutes, gradually increasing the speed, until the batter is light and foamy.
Replace the wire whip with the flex edge beater. Use the sifter and scale attachment to sift the flour and baking powder, then add to the bowl. Beat on speed 2 until all the flour has been incorporated. Add the butter while beating.

Let rest in the refrigerator for 2–3 hours.

Preheat a convection (fan-assisted) oven to 220°C - 425°F (gas mark 7). Brush the madeleine mold cavities with butter.
Put the batter in a pastry (piping) bag and pipe the batter into the cavities so that it reaches three-quarters of the way up. Let rest in the refrigerator for 1 hour.

Put into the oven and immediately reduce the oven temperature to 160°C - 325°F (gas mark 3). Bake for about 15 minutes.

VARIATIONS

You can make vanilla madeleines by substituting the lemon zest with vanilla powder.
You can also dip the underside of the madeleines in melted chocolate.

SHORT-BREAD

Makes 2 large shortbreads
or 12 small shortbreads

Preparation time: 20 minutes

Cooking time: 15-20 minutes

Resting time: 30 minutes

230 g butter, softened

**110 g superfine (caster)
sugar, plus 3 tbsp
for finishing**

230 g type-45 flour

100 g rice flour

Zest of 1 organic orange

1 pinch salt

Put the softened butter and the sugar in the bowl of
the mixer fitted with the flat beater. Beat on speed 2
for 1 minute, then on speed 4 for 2 minutes. Add the
flours, grated orange zest, and pinch of salt, and beat
on speed 4 for 3 minutes. It should come together in
a ball.

Divide the dough into two equal portions and lightly
flatten them with your hands to form two thick disks.
Reserve in the refrigerator for 30 minutes.

Preheat a convection (fan-assisted) oven to 160°C-325°F
(gas mark 3). Place each disk of dough onto a piece
of parchment (baking) paper. Use a rolling pin to roll
out the dough to a thickness of 8 mm and shape into
two 15-cm rectangles. Use the blade of a long knife to
score the surface to make a grid pattern. Prick with a
fork and sprinkle with sugar. Bake for 15–20 minutes.
The shortbreads should barely brown. Let cool on a
rack for a few minutes before cutting.

VARIATION

Flavor these cookies with
lemon zest or vanilla.

SCONES

500 g type-45 flour

11 g baking powder

1 pinch salt

60 g superfine (caster) sugar

125 g butter, softened

300 ml milk

1 egg yolk

Preheat the oven to 200°C - 400°F (gas mark 6).

Put the flour, baking powder, salt, and sugar into the bowl of the mixer fitted with the flat beater. Beat on speed 2 for 1 minute. Add the softened butter (cut into small cubes) and increase the speed to 4, beating for 1 minute. Finally, add the milk and beat for 2 minutes, until the dough comes together in a ball. The dough should be supple but not sticky.

Flour the work surface and use a rolling pin to roll out the dough to a thickness of 2–3 cm. Use a cookie cutter or a glass to cut disks of the dough 5–6 cm in diameter. Place them on a baking sheet lined with parchment (baking) paper. Brush the scones with egg yolk beaten with a little water to glaze them. Bake for 15–20 minutes. The scones should be nicely puffed and slightly golden.

Remove the scones from the oven and let cool on a rack. Serve them with clotted cream and jam.

TIP

You can add raisins to the dough. If you do, soak them beforehand in 1 tablespoon of rum mixed with a little water, or even in some tea.

VIENNESE BAGUETTES

Makes 2 baguettes

Preparation time: 15 minutes

Cooking time: 15 minutes

Resting time: 2 hours

100 ml low-fat (semi-skimmed) milk

10 g fresh baker's yeast

250 g type-45 flour

25 g superfine (caster) sugar

5 g salt

1 egg plus 1 egg yolk

35 g butter

Warm the milk, then pour it into the bowl of the mixer fitted with the dough hook. Add the crumbled yeast and mix on speed 2 for 2 minutes. Next, add the flour, sugar, salt, whole eggs, and softened butter (cut into cubes). Knead on speed 2 for 7–8 minutes. Cover with a dish cloth and let rise for 1 hour in a warm place.

Flour your hands and punch down the dough by kneading it lightly on a work surface. Shape into two long ropes. Place them on a baking sheet lined with parchment (baking) paper and let rise again for 1 hour.

Preheat the oven to 200°C - 400°F (gas mark 6). Score the top of the baguettes several times with the tip of a knife. Using a brush, glaze with the egg yolk beaten with a little water. Bake for 15 minutes. Enjoy the bread warm or toasted for breakfast.

basics

TIP

For gourmet baguettes, add chocolate chips to the dough after you finish kneading, mixing them in on speed 1 for 1 minute.

BANANA BREAD

**2 large ripe bananas
plus 1 for decorating**

130 g butter

100 g brown sugar

2 eggs

250 g type-45 flour

11 g baking powder

120 g chocolate chips

11 g vanilla sugar

Preheat the oven to 180°C - 350°F (gas mark 4).

Peel the bananas and cut them into rounds. Put them into the bowl of the mixer with the flex edge beater and puree the bananas on speed 2 for 1 minute. Melt the butter. Increase the speed to 4 and add the brown sugar, eggs, and then the melted butter. Immediately add the flour and baking powder and beat for 2 minutes. Lower the speed to 1, add the chocolate chips, and beat for 30 seconds.

Butter and flour a loaf pan and pour in the batter. Peel the remaining banana and cut it lengthwise. Place on top of the batter and sprinkle with the vanilla sugar. Bake for 1 hour. Let cool before unmolding.

TIPS

Make sure you use very ripe bananas for this recipe. You could vary the recipe by using caramel chips.

PECAN BROWNIES

Serves 6

Preparation time: 10 minutes

Cooking time: 30 minutes

200 g dark chocolate

200 g salted butter

4 eggs

160 g superfine (caster) sugar

80 g type-45 flour

1 tsp baking powder

100 g pecans, chopped

Preheat the oven to 180°C - 350°F (gas mark 4). Melt the chocolate and butter in a bain-marie.

Put the eggs and sugar into the bowl of the mixer fitted with the flex edge beater and mix on speed 4 for 1 minute. Add the melted chocolate and butter and mix for 1 minute. Add the flour and baking powder and mix for 2 minutes. Lower to speed 1 and add the chopped pecans.

Line a mold with parchment (baking) paper. Pour in the batter and bake for about 30 minutes. When done, let cool and then unmold.

TIPS

Pistachios, hazelnuts, almonds, walnuts pine nuts, vary the deliciousness! For a gluten-free version, substitute the wheat flour with rice flour.

RASPBERRY AND LEMON CAKE

Serves 8

Preparation time: 15 minutes

Cooking time: 45 minutes

180 g all-purpose (plain) flour

70 g almond meal (ground almonds)

150 g superfine (caster) sugar

1 tsp baking powder

1 pinch salt

125 g plain (natural) yogurt

2 eggs

60 ml neutral oil (peanut or canola/rapeseed)

1 lemon

300 g fresh raspberries

Preheat the oven to 180°C - 350°F (gas mark 6).

Put the flour, almond meal (ground almonds), sugar, baking powder, and salt into the bowl of the mixer fitted with the flex edge beater and beat on speed 1 for 1 minute. Add the yogurt, eggs, oil, juice, and grated lemon zest and beat on speed 4 for 3 minutes.

Butter and flour a 22 or 24-cm-diameter cake pan. Pour in the batter and arrange the fresh raspberries on top in rows. Bake for 45 minutes. When done, let the cake cool for 5 minutes before unmolding it onto a rack.

TIP

You can substitute the lemon with 1 tablespoon of pistachio paste and some chopped pistachios.

WAFFLES

Makes 15 waffles

Preparation time: 10 minutes

Cooking time: 10 minutes

250 g type-45 flour

11 g baking powder

40 g superfine (caster) sugar

50 g butter

2 eggs

500 ml milk

1 tsp vanilla extract

Confectioner's (icing) sugar

Put the flour, baking powder, and sugar into the bowl of the mixer fitted with the whisk attachment and mix on speed 2 for 30 seconds. Melt the butter. Add the eggs, milk, melted butter, and the vanilla extract. Mix on speed 4 for 1 minute, then on speed 8 for 3 minutes, being careful to use the pouring shield to prevent splashing.

Heat a waffle iron. When hot, pour in the batter and close it. Let cook for a few minutes, keeping an eye on them. The waffles should be nice and golden. When done, transfer to a plate and repeat until you have used all the batter. Sprinkle with confectioners' (icing) sugar and serve.

VARIATION

You can add 100 g granulated sugar to the batter; this will caramelize lightly during cooking and make the waffles even more tasty.

CHOCOLATE PEANUT COOKIES

Makes 25 cookies

Preparation time: 15 minutes

Cooking time: 12 minutes

200 g dark chocolate

100 g unsalted peanuts

200 g very soft butter

100 g superfine (caster) sugar

150 g brown sugar

2 eggs

370 g type-45 flour

11 g baking powder

1 tsp baking (bicarbonate of) soda

1 pinch fleur de sel

Preheat the oven to 180°C - 350°F (gas mark 4) on the convection (fan-assisted) setting. Coarsely chop the chocolate and peanuts with a knife.

In the bowl of the mixer fitted with the flex edge beater, mix the softened butter, superfine (caster) sugar, and brown sugar on speed 4 for 1 minute. Add the eggs and mix for 30 seconds. Gradually add the flour, baking powder, baking (bicarbonate of) soda, and fleur de sel. Mix on speed 4 for 2 minutes. Add the chopped chocolate and peanuts and mix on speed 1 for 30 seconds.

Form the dough into balls and arrange them on a baking sheet lined with parchment (baking) paper, leaving space between them. Flatten them slightly with the palm of your hand. Bake for 12 minutes, then check the cookies—they should be just beginning to brown. Let cool for 10 minutes before removing them from the parchment paper.

TIPS & VARIATIONS

To make the dough balls the same size, use an ice cream scoop.
You can flavor these cookies by replacing 100 g of the flour with hazelnut flour (ground hazelnuts).
Try using different nuts: almonds, pecans, hazelnuts, pine nuts, pistachios, etc.

CHOCOLATE MOUSSE

Serves 4

Preparation time: 15 minutes

Resting time: 4 hours minimum

180 g dark baking chocolate

60 g cream

60 g milk

1 pinch salt

3 large eggs

25 g superfine (caster) sugar

Break the chocolate into pieces and put into a bowl. In a saucepan, bring the cream and milk to a boil, then immediately pour over the chocolate. Mix well to melt all the chocolate pieces, then add the pinch of salt.

Separate the egg whites and yolks. Quickly whip the yolks.
Put the whites into the bowl of the mixer fitted with the wire whip. Start the mixer on a low speed, then gradually and incrementally increase the speed. Whip on speed 10 for about 1 minute 30 seconds, pouring in the sugar so the whipped egg whites become firm. Stop the mixer when the eggs begin to look like meringue. Use a rubber spatula to gently fold in the whipped egg yolks, then add the melted chocolate, being careful to avoid deflating the egg whites.
Refrigerate for at least 4 hours to let the mousse set and acquire a good texture.

TIP & VEGAN VERSION

To make a completely vegan version, simply use equal parts aquafaba (the drained liquid from the can of chickpeas) and chocolate by weight. Whip the aquafaba just as you would egg whites, add 25 g sugar, melt the chocolate in a double boiler, add a little salt, and combine gently. If you have some leftover chocolate and you like little pieces that melt in your mouth, don't hesitate to use a peeler to shave off flakes to sprinkle over the top of the mousse!

CHOCOLATE FONDANT

Serves 4-6

Preparation time: 10 minutes

Cooking time: 20 minutes

200 g dark chocolate

100 g salted butter

4 eggs

100 g demerara sugar

**50 g almond meal
(ground almonds)**

6 g baking powder

Preheat the oven to 200°C - 400°F (gas mark 6).

Melt the chocolate with the butter in the microwave or in a double boiler (bain-marie).

In the bowl of the mixer fitted with the flat beater, mix the eggs with the sugar on speed 4 for 2 minutes. Add the melted chocolate and butter and mix on speed 2 for 1 minute. Add the almond meal (ground almonds) and baking powder and mix on speed 2 for 1 minute.

Butter and flour a 24–25-cm-diameter cake pan. Pour in the batter and bake for 20 minutes. Serve warm with a scoop of frozen yogurt (see p. 316).

TIPS

Replace the almond meal with hazelnut flour (ground hazelnuts) or coconut flour. Add a pinch of fleur de sel to bring out the flavor.

CREPES
WITH SALTED
CARAMEL

CARAMEL

200 g sugar

100 g salted butter

4 tbsp Mascarpone cheese

CREPES

250 g type-45 flour

1 pinch salt

2 tbsp sugar

3 eggs

500 ml milk

CARAMEL
Put the sugar and 2 tbsp water into a small saucepan. Cook over medium heat until just caramelized. Cut the butter into small cubes and whisk the butter into the caramel. Finally, add the mascarpone cheese and mix. Pour into a bowl and let cool.

CREPES
In the bowl of the mixer fitted with the flex edge beater, mix the flour, salt, and sugar on speed 2. Add the eggs, one by one, then the milk. Whip on speed 2 for 2 minutes. Let stand for 30 minutes.

Heat a nonstick skillet or frying pan over high heat, buttering it lightly. When hot, ladle in a little batter. After a few minutes, flip the crepe and cook for 1–2 minutes. Transfer to a plate and repeat until all the batter has been used. Serve with the caramel spread

TIPS

You can replace the milk with a non-dairy milk (rice or almond milk) and the wheat flour with a gluten-free mix: 180 g rice flour and 70 g cornstarch (cornflour). You can flavor the batter with orange flower water, vanilla sugar, rum, etc.

FRESH
PREP

ENERGY JUICE

Serves 2

Preparation time: 5 minutes

2 apples

2 oranges

2 carrots

5 cm fresh ginger root

Wash the fruits, carrots, and the ginger. Quarter the apples and remove the seeds. Peel and quarter the oranges. Cut the carrots into chunks. Peel the ginger.

Juice the fruits, carrots, and ginger with the sauce attachment fitted with the fine pulp screen. Mix. Serve immediately.

TIP

For a sweeter version, add the juice of a pear. You can reserve the resulting pulp and use it when making cake or pancakes.

GREEN JUICE

1/2 cucumber

1 small bulb fennel

2 kale leaves

2 green apples

1/2 lemon

Wash the fruits and vegetables. Trim off the ends of the cucumber and cut it into quarters. Trim the fennel, if necessary, and cut it into large cubes. Chop the kale leaves into three or four pieces. Quarter the apples and remove the seeds. Peel the lemon with a knife.

Juice the fruits and vegetables with the sauce attachment fitted with the fine pulp screen. Mix. Serve immediately.

TIPS

Use organic fruits and vegetables, if possible. You can also add a little fresh turmeric to this juice.

DRAINING JUICE

Serves 2

Preparation time: 5 minutes

1 large raw beet (beetroot)

1 large bulb fennel

2 Reinette apples

Peel the beet (beetroot) and fennel, then wash the apples and remove their seeds. Cut the fruit and vegetables into large pieces.

Juice the fruit and vegetables with the sauce attachment fitted with the fine pulp screen. Serve immediately.

TIPS

Substitute radishes for the beet (beetroot) to make a spicy cocktail. You can also add the juice of 1/2 lemon.

ANTIOXIDANT
JUICE

Serves 2

Preparation time: 5 minutes

1 dozen strawberries

3 carrots

Juice of 1/2 lemon

Wash and hull the strawberries. Wash the carrots, cut off both ends, and chop into small chunks. Peel the lemon half.

Juice the fruits with the sauce attachment fitted with the fine pulp screen. Mix. Serve immediately.

TIP

You can also use blueberries, blackberries, pomegranates, or apples— these contain just as many antioxidants.

GUACAMOLE

3 ripe avocados

1 red onion

1 clove garlic

1 tbsp canned crushed tomato

1 tsp Tabasco® sauce

Juice of 1 lime

Salt

Pepper

Peel the red onion and garlic clove and cut them into quarters.
Discard the avocado skins and remove the pits.
Chop the red onion into cubes in the food processor attachment using the dicing disc and blade on speed 6. Cover with cold water and let soak for 30 minutes before draining.
Chop the avocados and garlic clove into cubes in the food processor attachment using the dicing disc and blade on speed 6.
Mix the avocados, red onion, garlic, tomato, Tabasco®, and lemon juice in a salad bowl; season with salt and pepper.
Serve cold.

TIPS

Perfect for an appetizer, you can also liven it up with fresh herbs (chives or cilantro/coriander). For a less spicy version, replace the Tabasco® with 1 tsp mild chili.

TZATZIKI

Serves 4

Preparation time: 5 minutes

125 g cucumber

1 clove garlic

250 g fromage frais or Greek yogurt

1 tbsp chopped chives

1 tbsp chopped flat-leaf parsley

2 pinches salt

Juice of 1/2 lemon

Cut the cucumber in half lengthwise and use a spoon to remove the seeds. Peel the garlic clove. Grate the cucumber and garlic clove using the Fresh Prep slicer/shredder fitted with the medium shredding blade on speed 6.
Put all of the ingredients into a salad bowl and mix gently.

Serve fresh with crudités or on individual toasts.

CUCUMBER GAZPACHO WITH SPICY CREAM

Serves 4

Preparation time: 10 minutes

2 cucumbers

1 zucchini (courgette)

2 small white onions

200 ml whipping cream

100 g Mascarpone cheese

1 tsp curry powder

Salt

Pepper

Wash the cucumbers and zucchini (courgette), then trim off the ends. Peel the onions. Puree into a soup using the sauce attachment fitted with the fine pulp screen on speed 4. Season with salt and pepper and pour into 4 glasses.

Put the cold whipping cream and the Mascarpone cheese into the bowl of the mixer fitted with the wire whip. Whip, gradually increasing the speed from 1 to 8. When the cream is whipped, add the salt and curry powder. Top each gazpacho with a dollop of whipped cream and serve immediately.

VARIATIONS

You can substitute 4 tbsp of fresh goat cheese for the Mascarpone cheese, softening it by whisking by hand before adding it to the whipped cream. You can also infuse your cream with a few basil leaves before letting it cool and whipping it. In this case, replace the curry powder with the zest of 1 lemon.

AVOCADO TOAST

Serves 2

Preparation time: 15 minutes

6 slices of bread

2 avocados

Juice of 1/2 lemon

Salt

Pepper

CUCUMBER AND SPROUTS TOAST

1/2 cucumber

2 tbsp leek sprouts

Drizzle of olive oil

Drizzle of lemon juice

APPLE AND SUNFLOWER SEED TOAST

1 apple

2 tbsp sunflower seeds

Drizzle of olive oil

Drizzle of lemon juice

PEAR AND GOAT CHEESE TOAST

1 pear

1 small piece goat cheese

1 tsp honey

Prepare the avocado: In the bowl of the mixer fitted with the flex edge beater, mix the avocado flesh with the lemon juice and a little salt on speed 4 for 2 minutes. Toast the slices of bread, then spread the avocado puree on top.

CUCUMBER AND SPROUTS TOAST
Peel the cucumber, then slice using the spiralizer with the fine spiralizing blade on speed 4. Place on two slices of bread, add the sprouts, and drizzle with olive oil and lemon juice. Season with salt and pepper.

APPLE AND SUNFLOWER SEED TOAST
Peel the apple using the spiralizer with the peeling blade, then slice using the fine spiralizing blade on speed 4. Place on two slices of bread, add the sunflower seeds, and drizzle with olive oil and lemon juice. Season with salt and pepper.

PEAR AND GOAT CHEESE TOAST
Peel the pear using the spiralizer with the peeling blade, then slice using the slicing blade (large or small core) on speed 4. Place on two slices of bread, add a few small pieces of goat cheese, and drizzle with a little honey. Season with salt and pepper.

Serve these toasts immediately.

TIPS

If you want to add more protein, you can add a few slices of smoked salmon to these toasts, or even a poached egg.

VEGGIE ROLLS

VEGGIE ROLLS

1 cucumber

1 nest rice vermicelli noodles

1 fennel bulb

2 carrots

Juice of 1 lemon

Salt

FETA-PISTACHIO SAUCE

50 g pistachios

125 g Greek yogurt

80 g feta cheese

1 tbsp olive oil

Salt

Pepper

Wash the cucumber, trim off the ends, then cut into four pieces of equal size. Use the vegetable sheet cutter on speed 2 to slice into thin sheets. Cut into strips about 15 cm long.

Cover the rice noodles with hot water and let stand for 5 minutes. Peel and trim the fennel and carrots, then cut into a medium julienne using the Fresh Prep slicer/shredder on speed 4. Sprinkle with lemon juice, season with salt, and mix.

Place a small amount of vermicelli and julienned vegetables at one end of one of the cucumber strips. Roll up the cucumber to make an attractive roll.

Make the sauce: Chop the pistachios with the Fresh Prep slicer/shredder fitted with the medium shredding blade on speed 4. Put the chopped pistachios into the bowl of the mixer fitted with the flex edge beater and add the Greek yogurt, feta cheese, olive oil, salt, and pepper. Mix on speed 4.

Serve the rolls cold with the sauce.

TIPS

You can replace the rice vermicelli with sprouts. Vary the vegetables according to the season and your preferences; you can add slices of button mushroom, asparagus, shredded red cabbage, palm heart, etc.

APPLE, BEET, AND COMTÉ CARPACCIO

1 apple

2 beets, cooked

70 g Comté cheese

VINAIGRETTE

3 tbsp walnut oil

1 tbsp white balsamic vinegar

Salt

Pepper

Make the vinaigrette: In a bowl, mix the oil, vinegar, salt, and pepper. Emulsify with a spoon, then set aside.

Peel the apple. One by one, cut the beets, apple, and Comté cheese into fine slices using the food processor attachment on speed 4 with the slicing disc set to the minimum size. Arrange them on the plates, alternating each ingredient. Drizzle with a few drops of vinaigrette. Serve immediately or keep refrigerated.

TIPS

You can add a few walnuts or pine nuts. You can also replace the apple with pear.

ZUCCHINI, AND RICOTTA (GLUTEN-FREE) BLINIS

Serves 4

Preparation time: 10 minutes

Cooking time: 10 minutes

BLINIS

2 zucchini (courgettes)

2 eggs

2 tbsp cornstarch (cornflour)

150 g ricotta cheese

Salt

Pepper

TOPPING

100 g ricotta cheese

Chives

Zest of 1 lemon

BLINIS

Wash the zucchini (courgettes) and cut off the ends. Use the food processor attachment with the julienne disc to slice them on speed 4.
Put the eggs, cornstarch (cornflour), ricotta, salt, and pepper into the bowl of the mixer fitted with the flat beater and mix on speed 4 for 2 minutes. Add the julienned zucchini and mix on speed 1 for 1 minute.

Lightly oil a skillet or frying pan, then pour in small amounts of the batter, spacing them well apart. After a few minutes, check to see if the undersides are done and, if so, turn them over. When done, transfer to a plate and repeat until you have used all the batter.

Spread a little ricotta onto each blini and sprinkle with chopped chives and a little grated lemon zest. Serve immediately.

VARIATION

If you wish, you can add a little salmon roe to the ricotta cheese.

THIN SUMMER VEGETABLE TART

Serves 6

Preparation time: 10 minutes

Cooking time: 40 minutes

Resting time: 30 minutes

Make the puff pastry as described on p. 37.

Preheat the oven to 180°C - 350°F (gas mark 4). Roll the dough onto a sheet of parchment (baking) paper to make a large disk about 40 cm in diameter. If desired, decorate the edges attractively. In a bowl, mix together the ricotta cheese, mustard, and olive oil, then add salt and pepper. Spread this mixture over the dough, being careful to leave a border all around the edge of the tart.

Wash the zucchini (courgettes), trim off the ends, then cut in half lengthwise. Cut into fine slices using the food processor attachment on speed 4 with the slicing disc set to the minimum size. Distribute the slices over the tart. Add a few quartered cherry tomatoes. Wash and chop the basil, then distribute over the tart. Season with salt and pepper. Bake for 35–40 minutes. The edges of the tart should be golden brown.

PUFF PASTRY

250 g type-45 flour

200 g butter

5 g salt

120 ml water

TOPPING

4 tbsp ricotta cheese

1 tbsp whole-grain mustard

1 tbsp olive oil

3 zucchini (courgettes)

Cherry tomatoes

Basil leaves

Salt

Pepper

VARIATIONS

You can replace the ricotta cheese with fresh goat cheese or even with tapenade or pesto.
For a gluten-free version, replace the wheat flour with 150 g rice flour and 50 g cornstarch (cornflour).

RAW VEGETABLE SALAD
WITH PINE NUTS

Serves 4

Preparation time: 10 minutes

2 carrots

1/2 celery root (celeriac)

1 large zucchini (courgette)

50 g pine nuts

1 tsp apple cider vinegar

3 tbsp olive oil

1 tsp honey

Salt

Pepper

Put the pine nuts into a small skillet or frying pan and toast them dry (without oil or grease) for a few minutes.

Peel the carrots and the half celery root (celeriac), wash the zucchini, and use the food processor attachment with the julienne disc to slice them on speed 4.

Mix the vinegar, oil, and honey in a salad bowl. Season with salt and pepper, then beat with a fork. Add the sliced vegetables and mix well. Add the toasted pine nuts immediately before serving.

TIP

To give this salad an Asian twist, you can add raisins, a little quatre-épices spice blend, and chopped cilantro (coriander).

POTATO
AND VEGETABLE
ROSTI

Serves 4

Preparation time: 10 minutes

Cooking time: 45 minutes

4 potatoes

2 carrots

1 zucchini (courgette)

2 cloves garlic

1 tbsp oil

2 eggs

2 tbsp crème fraîche

1 tbsp chopped chives

Salt

Pepper

Preheat the oven to 180°C - 350°F (gas mark 4).

Peel the potatoes, carrots, zucchini, and garlic cloves, then use the food processor attachment with the julienne disc to slice them on speed 4. Put the sliced vegetables into a saucepan with the oil and cook for 15 minutes, stirring often.

Put the eggs, crème fraîche, and chives into the bowl of the mixer fitted with the wire whip. Whip on speed 4 for 1 minute. Pour the mixture over the vegetables and use a spatula to mix gently. Generously butter a round cake pan and pour in the mixture. Bake for 30–35 minutes, keeping a close eye on the cake. It should be a deep golden brown.

VARIATIONS

Use different vegetables and herbs, depending on the season: leeks, celery, and parsnips in the winter, and zucchini and peas in the summer. You can also add corn kernels.

COLESLAW

Serves 4–6

Preparation time: 10 minutes

Resting time: 30 minutes

2 carrots

1/2 white cabbage

1 egg yolk

1 tbsp mustard

1 tsp wine vinegar

150–250 ml peanut oil

2 tbsp yogurt

Salt

Pepper

Make the mayonnaise: In the bowl of the mixer fitted with the wire whip, mix the egg yolk, mustard, and vinegar on speed 4 for 1 minute. Increase the speed to 6 and add the oil in a thin stream until a good mayonnaise forms. Season with salt and pepper and let stand in the refrigerator.

Peel the carrots and trim the cabbage, then chop both into large pieces. Use the food processor attachment fitted with the julienne disc to slice them on speed 4.

In a bowl, mix the yogurt with 3 tbsp of the mayonnaise. Add this sauce to the raw vegetables and mix. Cover the salad bowl with plastic wrap (clingfilm) and refrigerate for 30 minutes. Serve with homemade sandwiches.

fresh
prep

VARIATIONS

Try using other vegetables: parsnips, raw beets (beetroot), celery root (celeriac), etc.

VEGETABLE NOODLES
WITH CREAM SAUCE AND SUN-DRIED TOMATOES

Serves 2

Preparation time: 5 minutes

Cooking time: 20 minutes

2 carrots

2 parsnips

1 clove garlic

50 ml light (single) cream

50 g sun-dried tomatoes

30 g grated Parmesan cheese

1 dozen basil leaves

Olive oil

Salt

Pepper

Peel the carrots and parsnips. Slice them into spaghetti-like strands using the spiralizer on speed 2. Peel the garlic clove and chop finely.

Heat the olive oil in a saucepan. Add the vegetable spaghetti, then add the cream, sun-dried tomatoes, and Parmesan cheese. Season with salt and pepper, add 1/2 cup water, cover, and simmer over low heat for 20 minutes, stirring often.

Just before serving, chop and add the basil. Serve immediately.

TIPS

Parsnips are a winter vegetable; in the summer months, replace them with zucchini (courgettes). You can also add olives to this dish.

RATATOUILLE

Serves 4-6

Preparation time: 15 minutes

Cooking time: 35 minutes

2 onions

2 cloves garlic

A drizzle of olive oil

1 red bell pepper

2 zucchini (courgettes)

1 eggplant (aubergine)

4 tomatoes

Thyme

Salt

Pepper

Peel the onions and garlic cloves. Cut them into cubes in the food processor attachment using the dicing disc on speed 6. Brown in a deep skillet or frying pan with olive oil over low heat for 5 minutes.

Next, chop the red pepper, zucchini (courgettes), and eggplant (aubergine) on speed 4. Add to the pan.

Cut the tomatoes into quarters and make a coulis using the fruit and vegetable strainer. Add to the pan. Season with salt and pepper, add the thyme, and stir. Simmer for 30 minutes.

Serve hot or cold.

TIP

You can also add rosemary, bay leaves, oregano, basil, etc.

FRENCH-STYLE STEWED VEGETABLES

Serves 4

Preparation time: 10 minutes

Cooking time: 30 minutes

4 carrots

2 large potatoes

100 g celery root (celeriac)

2 onions

100 g bacon

150 g sweet peas (petits pois), frozen or fresh

1 sprig thyme

2 bay leaves

1 tsp sugar

1 chicken bouillon (stock) cube

Salt

Pepper

Peel the carrots, potatoes, celery root (celeriac), and onions. First, cut the onions into cubes in the food processor attachment using the dicing disc on speed 6. Put into a pot or Dutch oven (cast iron casserole) with the bacon and brown over high heat for 5 minutes.

Cut the carrots, potatoes, and celery root (celeriac) into cubes similar to the onions, then add them to the pot along with the sweet peas (petits pois). Add enough water to cover, then add the thyme, bay leaves, sugar, bouillon (stock) cube, salt, and pepper. Simmer for 30 minutes over low heat.

Serve with roasted meat.

VARIATIONS

Use different vegetables depending on the season: in spring, add baby turnips or fava (broad) beans. In summer, add green beans cut into small pieces.

VEGGIE BURGER

Serves 6

Preparation time: 30 minutes

Cooking time: 25 minutes

Resting time:
2 hours 15 minutes

BURGER BUNS
Make the burger buns as described on p. 32.

VEGGIE BURGERS
Drain, rinse, and dry the chickpeas. Quarter the red bell pepper and remove its seeds. Peel the garlic and onion. Using the food grinder with the coarse plate, grind the chickpeas with the red bell pepper, garlic, and onion. Transfer the mixture to the bowl of the mixer fitted with the flat beater. Add the quinoa, beaten egg, and salt, then mix on speed 2 for 2 minutes.

Heat the olive oil in a skillet or frying pan. Pack one-sixth of the mixture into the bottom of a small bowl to form a patty, then add it to the skillet. Repeat five times to make the other patties. Cook for 5 minutes, then flip and cook for another 5 minutes on the other side.

TOPPING
Slice the buns in half. Peel the avocados and cut them into slices. Set the veggie burgers on the buns and add the avocado and lettuce. Replace the tops of the buns and serve hot.

BURGER BUNS

300 g flour

5 g active dry yeast

20 g butter

5 g salt

15 g sugar

70 ml milk

1 egg, beaten

1 egg yolk

40 g sesame seeds

VEGGIE BURGERS

300 g chickpeas (canned or jarred)

1 red bell pepper

1 clove garlic

1 onion

200 g cooked quinoa

1 egg, beaten

Salt

1 tbsp olive oil

TOPPING

2 avocados

A few lettuce leaves

VARIATIONS

For a spicy version, add cumin and paprika to your burgers. You can also add aromatic herbs, such as cilantro (coriander), parsley, etc.
Use different toppings: Tomato slices, sprouts, vegetable slices, etc.

ASIAN TOFU SALAD

Serves 4

Preparation time: 10 minutes

Cooking time: 8 minutes

200 g smoked tofu

1 cucumber

4 carrots

150 g iceberg lettuce

1/2 bunch cilantro (coriander)

100 g soybean sprouts

Juice of 1 lime

3 tbsp soy sauce

3 tbsp neutral oil

2 tbsp sesame oil

1 tbsp sesame seeds

Salt

Pepper

Peel the cucumber and carrots, then slice using the spiralizer with the fine spiralizing blade on speed 4. Wash the lettuce, then cut into strips. Strip off the cilantro (coriander) leaves and chop. In a large bowl, combine the carrots, cucumber, lettuce, cilantro leaves, and soybean sprouts.

In a bowl, mix the lime juice, soy sauce, 2 tbsp neutral oil, sesame oil, salt, and pepper.

Cut the tofu into small cubes. Heat the remaining oil in a skillet or frying pan, then brown the tofu for 7–8 minutes, stirring often. Add to the vegetables in the large bowl, pour in the dressing, sprinkle with sesame seeds, mix, and serve immediately.

TIPS

For a salad with a little more kick, add 1 tsp Tabasco® to the dressing. You can replace the sesame seeds with sunflower seeds or even crushed peanuts.

ZUCCHINI ROLLS
WITH COD, BELL PEPPERS, AND BEURRE BLANC

Serves 4 / Makes 12 rolls

Preparation time: 20 minutes

Cooking time: 35 minutes

ZUCCHINI ROLLS

2 red bell peppers

1 onion

1 tbsp olive oil

4 zucchini (courgettes)

500 g salted cod, desalted

Salt

Pepper

BEURRE BLANC

1 shallot

1 tbsp white vinegar

50 ml white wine

100 g butter

Salt

ZUCCHINI ROLLS

Wash the red bell peppers, then cut in half and remove the seeds. Peel and quarter the onion. Cut into cubes in the food processor attachment using the dicing disc on speed 6. Brown, covered, with the olive oil in a skillet or frying pan over low heat for 20 minutes. If necessary, add a little water. The red bell peppers should be soft.

Wash the zucchini (courgettes), trim off the ends, then cut in half, if necessary. Use the vegetable sheet cutter on speed 2 to slice into thick sheets. Cut into 12 strips about 15 cm long. Cut the cod into 12 rectangular pieces. Place a little cooked red bell pepper along the edge of one of the strips, then add a piece of fish. Roll the zucchini around the fish to make a roll. Repeat with the remaining 11 zucchini strips. Place the rolls in a steamer basket and cook for 10 minutes.

BEURRE BLANC

Peel the shallot, then chop finely. Combine with the vinegar in a saucepan and reduce over high heat, stirring constantly. Next, add the white wine to deglaze the pan. Finally, gradually add the butter in small cubes, whisking constantly to emulsify the sauce. Season with salt, then strain through a fine conical strainer.

Serve the rolls with the beurre blanc and, optionally, with basmati rice.

TIPS

You can replace the cod with a different white fish. You can add tomato and chopped cilantro (coriander) to the pan with the red bell pepper; you can also add a pinch of curry powder to the beurre blanc.

ZUCCHINI SALAD WITH GOAT CHEESE

Serves 4

Preparation time: 10 minutes

2 zucchini (courgettes)

1/2 bunch cilantro (coriander)

1 tsp white balsamic vinegar

2 tbsp olive oil

1 pinch curry powder

2 tbsp fresh goat cheese

Salt

Freshly ground pepper

Wash the cilantro (coriander) and chop finely.

Wash the zucchini (courgettes) and trim off the ends. Slice the zucchini into spaghetti-like strainds using the spiralizer on speed 2.

Put the vinegar, oil, curry powder, salt, pepper, and goat cheese into a salad bowl. Mix well and add the chopped cilantro. Finally, add the spiralized zucchini, mix, and serve cold.

VARIATIONS

You can replace the cilantro with mint and the curry with cumin; you can also substitute Roquefort for the goat cheese and add walnuts.

ORANGE AND CARROT SALAD
WITH ORANGE FLOWER WATER

Serves 4

Preparation time: 10 minutes

Resting time: 1 hour

400 g carrots

2 oranges

1 tsp orange flower water

1 tbsp superfine (caster) sugar

2 tbsp olive oil

1 tbsp sesame seeds

Salt

Peel the carrots and chop them coarsely. Use the food processor attachment fitted with the shredding disc to shred them on speed 4.

Use the citrus juicer on speed 6 to extract the juice of half an orange. Pour into a bowl, then add the orange flower water, sugar, olive oil, and a pinch of salt. Mix and pour over the carrots.

Peel the remaining oranges and section them using a knife, being careful to remove the white pith and the membranes. Add the orange sections to the salad, sprinkle with the sesame seeds, and refrigerate for 1 hour before serving.

TIP

You can add chopped cilantro (coriander) or mint, cinnamon, raisins, toasted pumpkin seeds, etc.

PAVLOVA

MERINGUE

3 egg whites

55 g confectioners' (icing) sugar

55 g superfine (caster) sugar

50 g shelled green pistachios

TOPPING

250 ml whipping cream (250 g)

40 g confectioners' (icing) sugar

Berries (strawberries, raspberries, red currants, blueberries, etc.)

Preheat the oven to 120°C - 250°F (gas mark 1/2). Put the egg whites into the bowl of the mixer fitted with the wire whip. Whip, starting on speed 1 and gradually increasing the speed to 8. When soft peaks form, add the confectioners' (icing) sugar and superfine (caster) sugar. When the meringue is glossy, make four mounds on a baking sheet lined with parchment (baking) paper. Flatten them slightly with the back of a spoon. Sprinkle with the chopped pistachios and bake for 1 hour 15 minutes. When done, let cool.

Whip the cold whipping cream with the confectioners' (icing) sugar in the bowl of the mixer fitted with the wire whip gradually increasing the speed from 1 to 10 to make a Chantilly cream. Spoon the Chantilly cream over the meringues and top with the berries.

TIP

You can also make pretty meringue spirals by piping the meringue onto the baking sheet using a pastry (piping) bag with a plain tip.

L E M O N
S O R B E T

Serves 4

Preparation time: 10 minutes

Resting time: 1 hour
25 minutes

3 lemons

200 g sugar

2 egg whites

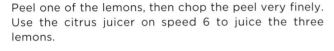

Peel one of the lemons, then chop the peel very finely. Use the citrus juicer on speed 6 to juice the three lemons.

Put the sugar, 500 ml water, lemon juice, and lemon zest into a saucepan. Heat over low heat until the sugar dissolves. Let cool for 1 hour.

Whip the egg whites until they form stiff peaks using the mixer fitted with the wire whip, raising the speed gradually from 1 to 6, then fold them together gently with the lemon syrup. Start the ice cream maker on speed 4 and pour in the mixture. Churn the sorbet for 25 minutes. Keep in the freezer.

TIPS

You can replace the lemons with limes, oranges, or grapefruit. When serving, crush 150 g meringues and sprinkle them over the sorbet.

SMOOTHIE BOWL

SMOOTHIE

1 large apple

1/2 banana

50 g raspberries

**2 tbsp fromage frais
or Greek yogurt**

TOPPING

**Assorted fresh fruits:
blueberries, raspberries,
bananas**

**Nuts: hazelnuts, walnuts,
almonds**

**Seeds: sesame, poppy,
or some muesli**

Wash the apple, then quarter it and remove the seeds. Peel the banana. Juice the apple, banana, and raspberries with the sauce attachment fitted with the coarse pulp screen. Add the fromage frais or Greek yogurt to the juice, mix, and transfer to a bowl.

Add your toppings: fruits, nuts, and seeds. Serve immediately.

TIPS

For a lactose-free version, use soy (soya) yogurt.

CARIBBEAN PUNCH

Serves 4

Preparation time: 15 minutes

4 oranges

2 grapefruits

2 pineapples

160 ml rum

50 ml cane sugar

Crushed ice

Peel the oranges and grapefruit. Trim the pineapples and discard the woody core. Cut all the fruits into pieces. Juice them in the sauce attachment fitted with the fine pulp screen on speed 4. Collect the juice, add the rum and cane sugar, and mix.

Fill four glasses with crushed ice and pour in the punch. Serve cold.

VARIATIONS

Not interested in rum? Replace it with the juice from 2 passionfruits—cut them in half, scrape out the pulp, and juice it using the sauce attachment on speed 2.
Use different exotic fruits to create an infinite variety of punches.

STRAWBERRY DAIQUIRI

Serves 4

Preparation time: 5 minutes

500 g strawberries

3 limes

160 ml Cuban rum

100 ml cane sugar syrup

Ice cubes

Wash and hull the strawberries and peel the limes. Juice the strawberries and limes in the sauce attachment fitted with the fine pulp screen on speed 4.
Collect the juice, add the rum and sugar syrup, and mix.

Distribute the ice cubes among four glasses and pour in the strawberry daiquiri. Serve immediately while cold.

TIPS

Buy a few extra strawberries and place a strawberry in each glass before serving.
For a virgin cocktail, omit the rum and add 100 g strawberries and 1 lime.

PIÑA
COLADA

Serves 3–4

Preparation time: 15 minutes

1 (1-kg) pineapple

200 ml white rum

200 ml coconut cream

Juice of 1 lemon, plus 1 tbsp

50 g unsweetened dried shredded coconut

Cut off the top and bottom of the pineapple. Turning the pineapple, use a large knife to trim away the skin. Use the tip of a vegetable peeler to remove the "eyes," then quarter the pineapple vertically down the center. Discard the woody core. Cut the flesh into pieces. Juice the pineapple using the sauce attachment fitted with the fine pulp screen. Add the rum, coconut cream, and lemon juice. Mix.

Pour 1 tablespoon of lemon juice into a saucer. Place the dried coconut on a small plate. Dip the rim of each glass into the lemon juice, then the coconut.

Without disturbing the rim, carefully pour the drink into the glasses and serve immediately.

TIPS

Coconut cream, which is thicker and richer than coconut milk, is sold in 250-ml blocks. You can add sugar syrup (about 1 tbsp per person) or make a virgin version.

MEAT & SAVORY

CREAM

OF BUTTERNUT SQUASH, GINGER-LEMON CHANTILLY

Serves 4

Preparation time: 15 minutes

Cooking time: 40 minutes

500 g butternut squash

20 g shallot

Olive oil

600 ml water

1/2 vegetable bouillon (stock) cube

150 ml cream

1 tsp curry powder

1 small piece fresh ginger (1 g)

A little lemon zest

Salt (optional)

Pepper

Wash and peel the squash. If organic, you don't need to peel it. Halve it lengthwise. Cut the lower section into halves or quarters and remove the seeds. Cut the flesh into large pieces.

Peel and finely chop the shallots. Heat a little olive oil in a Dutch oven (cast-iron casserole). Sweat the shallots over medium heat for 2–3 minutes.

In the meantime, heat the water. Add the pieces of squash, ½ bouillon (stock) cube, and hot water. Cover and cook for about 20 minutes or until the squash is tender.
Add 40 ml of the cream and the curry powder, and season with pepper. Use the blender or handheld blender to blend. Season with salt, if necessary.

Use the rest of the cream to make whipped cream as described on p. 43, then grate in a little fresh ginger and the lemon zest. Stir, then add a little of the whipped cream to each soup bowl using a spoon or a pastry bag.

ALTERNATIVES

You can use any kind of squash for this recipe: pumpkin, ambercup squash, pattypan squash, etc. Use whatever you find locally.

SALMON TARTARE

Serves 4

Preparation time: 10 minutes

Resting time: 1 hour

300 g fresh salmon

1 red onion

1/2 mango

1 pinch ground ginger

Juice of 1 lime

15 chives

1 avocado

Salt

Peel the onion and mango. Cut them, along with the salmon, into cubes in the food processor attachment using the dicing disc on speed 4. Add the ground ginger and lime juice and stir. Let marinate for 1 hour in the refrigerator.

Before serving, finely chop the chives, cut the avocado into small dice with a knife, and add them to the tartare. Stir gently, then use a ring mold to place the right amount on each plate. Serve immediately.

VARIATION

Replace the mango with some small cubes of sour green apple.

HUMMUS

Serves 4-6

Preparation time: 5 minutes

**1 can chickpeas
(550 g drained)**

2 cloves garlic

100 ml olive oil

Juice of 1 lemon

1 pinch cumin

1 tsp tahini (optional)

Salt

Drain the chickpeas. Peel the garlic. Put the chickpeas and garlic into the mixer fitted with the fruit and vegetable strainer. Puree them on speed 4, gradually adding the olive oil and lemon juice.

Add the cumin and the tahini, if desired. Mix and adjust the seasoning. Store in the refrigerator and serve cold.

meat
& savory

TIPS

Add a little olive oil just before serving. You can replace the cumin with paprika. Tahini is a sesame paste that can be found at many health food stores.

TARAMA

Serves 4–6

Preparation time: 10 minutes

Resting time: 2 hours

160 g smoked cod's roe

35 g white bread

1/2 egg yolk (about 10 g)

2 tbsp milk

80 g oil

Cut the membrane of the cod's roe in half and scoop out the eggs. Set aside 160 g.

In the bowl of the stand mixer fitted with the flat beater, crumble in the bread, add the half egg yolk, and pour in the milk. Whip on speed 2. With the mixer running, pour in the oil in a fine stream. Add the cod's roe, steadily increasing the mixer speed. Beat on speed 8 for 3 minutes, then turn off the mixer.

Transfer to a bowl and refrigerate for 2 hours. Enjoy.

COUNTRY- STYLE TERRINE

Serves 6–8

Preparation time: 15 minutes

Cooking time: 1 hour 30 minutes

Resting time: 24–48 hours

250 g pork shoulder

100 g bacon

100 g chicken breast

80 g hazelnuts

10 sprigs flat-leaf parsley

1 onion

2 eggs

100 ml Martini® vermouth

1 sprig thyme

1 bay leaf

Salt

Pepper

Preheat the oven to 180°C - 350°F (gas mark 4). Coarsely chop the hazelnuts and mince the parsley. Peel the onion and chop the meats with a knife. Using the mixer fitted with the food grinder, grind (mince) the meats and onion on speed 6, using the fine plate. Transfer to the mixer bowl.

Add the hazelnuts, parsley, eggs, and vermouth and mix with the flex edge beater on speed 2 for 1 minute. Season with salt and pepper.

Transfer the mixture to a lidded baking dish. Place the thyme and bay leaf on top and cover with the lid. Bake for 1 hour 30 minutes. Let cool, then refrigerate for 24–48 hours, placing a weight on top of the terrine. Serve with well-toasted bread.

meat
& savory

VARIATIONS

You can add chicken liver to this terrine. For a slightly "richer" terrine, you can replace the chicken breasts with chicken thighs.

FALAFEL

Makes 12 falafel balls

Preparation time: 10 minutes

Cooking time: 3 minutes

Resting time: Overnight

The previous day, soak the chickpeas in a generous amount of water for 12–24 hours.

The next day, peel the onion and garlic. Wash the cilantro and parsley and discard the stems, then dry the leaves carefully. Drain the chickpeas, then dry them carefully. Using the food grinder with the fine plate, grind the chickpeas with the garlic, onion, and fresh herbs. In the bowl of the mixer fitted with the flex edge beater, mix the chickpea puree with the spices, baking (bicarbonate of) soda, sesame seeds, and salt. Mix on speed 2 for 2 minutes. Use your hands to form 12 balls the size of walnuts.

Heat the oil for deep-frying to 180°C - 350°F. Fry the falafels for about 3 minutes. They should be a deep golden brown. Drain on paper towels.

Mix the yogurt with the lemon juice and a pinch of salt. Serve the hot falafel with the sauce.

FALAFEL

300 g dry chickpeas

1 small onion

2 cloves garlic

1/2 bunch parsley

1/2 bunch cilantro (coriander)

1/2 tsp paprika

1/2 tsp ground cumin

1/2 tsp ground coriander

1 tsp baking (bicarbonate of) soda

2 tbsp sesame seeds

Salt

Oil for deep-frying

SAUCE

1 Greek yogurt

1 tbsp lemon juice

Salt

TIPS

For this recipe, it is important to use dry chickpeas, soaked overnight in water, and not canned chickpeas; these have too much water and will cause the falafel to explode when cooked.
You can replace half the chickpeas with dried fava (broad) beans, also soaked overnight in water.

ZUCCHINI FRITTATA

Serves 2

Preparation time: 5 minutes

Cooking time: 15 minutes

100 g zucchini (courgettes)

4 eggs

40 g grated Parmesan cheese

20 basil leaves

Olive oil

Salt

Pepper

Wash the zucchini (courgettes) and cut off the ends. Use the food processor attachment with the julienne disc to slice them on speed 4.

Put the eggs, Parmesan cheese, and finely sliced basil into the bowl of the mixer fitted with the wire whip and mix on speed 4 for 1 minute. Lower to speed 2 and add the julienned zucchini. Season with salt and pepper and continue to mix for 1 minute.

Heat a little olive oil in a medium skillet or frying pan. Pour in the mixture and cook over low heat for 10 minutes. Turn the frittata over and cook for another 5 minutes. Serve hot or cold.

VARIATION

You can substitute the Parmesan cheese with diced feta cheese, or even add sun-dried tomatoes, olives, curry, etc.

CHORIZO

Serves 4–6

Preparation time: 1 hour

Cooking time: 15–20 minutes

Resting time: 1 hour–
overnight, plus 30 minutes

500 g pork shoulder

100 g lard

2 cloves garlic

2 tbsp smoked paprika

1 tsp chili powder

1 tsp pepper

30 ml dry white wine

1/2 tbsp salt

1 m pig intestine

White vinegar

Wine vinegar

Peel the garlic.
Cut the meat into large chunks, then grind (mince) them with the garlic using the food grinder with the fine plate on speed 2.
Add the spices, white wine, and salt and mix well. Let stand in a cold place for at least 1 hour; if possible, let stand overnight for better flavor.

Meanwhile, rinse the pig intestine and soak it in water mixed with white vinegar for 30 minutes, changing the water often.
Clean the inside well by holding it open under running water.
Finally, pour a little wine vinegar through the intestine to keep its taste and smell from being too strong. Once the intestine has been well cleaned, attach it to the sausage stuffer, lightly oiling it beforehand.

Put the meat into the sausage stuffer. When the meat reaches the end of the intestine, turn off the mixer and knot or tie off the intestine. Turn the mixer back on at its lowest speed and continue to stuff the sausage until all stuffing has been used. Turn off the mixer and knot or tie off the other end of the intestine. Pierce any air bubbles with a toothpick (cocktail stick) or the point of a knife, then make the sausages by twisting the intestine over on itself.
Fry the sausage in a covered skillet or frying pan with a little fat for 15–20 minutes over medium heat. Serve with salad.

TIPS

It is easier to stuff sausages if you have a helper!
If you want to make a spicier chorizo, add 1 tbsp smoked paprika and 1 tsp chili powder.
These sausages freeze well.

SAUSAGES WITH HERBS

Serves 4-6

Preparation time: 1 hour

Cooking time: 15-20 minutes

Resting time: 1 hour–overnight, plus 30 minutes

600 g pork shoulder

100 g bacon

2 cloves garlic

½ tsp Espelette pepper

1 tsp brown sugar

1 tsp pepper

10 sprigs flat-leaf parsley

10 sprigs cilantro (coriander)

1 sprig thyme

1 m pig intestine

White vinegar

Wine vinegar

Peel the garlic.
Chop the meat into large chunks, then grind with the garlic using the food grinder with the fine plate on speed 2.
Add the spices and chopped herbs and mix well. Let stand for at least 1 hour in a cold place; if possible, let stand overnight for better flavor.

Meanwhile, rinse the intestine under running water, then soak in water mixed with vinegar for 30 minutes, changing the water often.
Clean the inside well by holding it open under running water.
Finally, pour a little wine vinegar through the intestine to keep its taste and smell from being too strong. Once the intestine has been well cleaned, attach it to the sausage stuffer, lightly oiling it beforehand.

Put the meat into the sausage stuffer. When the meat reaches the end of the intestine, turn off the mixer and knot or tie off the intestine. Turn the mixer back on at its lowest speed and continue to stuff the sausage until all the stuffing has been used. Turn off the mixer and knot or tie off the other end of the intestine. Pierce any air bubbles with a toothpick (cocktail stick) or the point of a knife.
Fry the sausage in a covered skillet or frying pan with a little fat for 15-20 minutes over medium heat.

TIPS

It is easier to stuff sausages if you have a helper!
If you want, you can make individual sausages by twisting the intestine over on itself.

STEAK TARTARE

Serves 4

Preparation time: 15 minutes

600 g steak

2 shallots

30 g capers

40 g mini pickles (cornichons)

1 small bunch parsley

1 tbsp Dijon mustard

3 drops Tabasco sauce

2 tbsp Worcestershire sauce

2 egg yolks

Salt

Pepper

Chop the steak using the mixer fitted with the food grinder with the fine plate on speed 2. Peel the shallots and grind; grind the capers and pickles. Wash and chop the parsley. Set aside.

Mix the meat with the shallots, capers, and pickles. Add the mustard, parsley, Tabasco, Worcestershire sauce, and egg yolks. Season with salt and pepper.

Divide among four plates. Serve with French fries.

TIPS

Tartare does not keep; serve immediately. You can grind the meat more or less finely according to taste.

CURRIED CHICKEN
BALLS

Serves 4

Preparation time: 15 minutes

Cooking time: 35 minutes

400 g chicken breast

1 onion

1 clove garlic

1 bunch cilantro (coriander)

1 egg white

Espelette pepper

Juice of 1/2 lemon

1 tbsp olive oil

1 tbsp curry powder

200 ml coconut milk

100 ml water

Salt

Pepper

Grind (mince) the chicken breasts with the mixer fitted with the food grinder on speed 2, using the fine plate. Peel the onion and garlic, then grind. Wash and chop half the cilantro (coriander).

Put the ground chicken, onion, garlic, egg white, chopped cilantro, a little Espelette pepper, and the lemon juice in the bowl of the mixer. Season with salt and pepper. Mix everything together with the flex edge beater on speed 4 for 1 minute.

Use your hands to make meatballs the size of a large walnut. Put them into a skillet or frying pan with a little olive oil and brown for 10 minutes. Sprinkle with curry powder. Dilute the coconut milk with 100 ml water and add the mixture to the pan. Season with salt and pepper and simmer for 25 minutes over low heat.
Add the rest of the cilantro just before serving. Serve hot with basmati rice.

MASHED POTATOES

Serves 4

Preparation time: 10 minutes

Cooking time: 30 minutes

800 g potatoes for mashing

150 ml milk

50 g butter

Salt

Cook the potatoes whole by either steaming or boiling them. Peel them, then heat the milk with the butter. Cut the potatoes into large chunks, then put them into the bowl of the mixer fitted with the flat beater. Mix on speed 2, gradually adding the milk and melted butter. Add a little salt and mix until the desired texture is reached. Serve hot.

TIP & VARIATIONS

Take care not to mix too much, as the mash may become rubbery.
You can replace the milk and butter with 2 tbsp of good-quality oil and add some crushed hazelnuts.
For a festive version, you can add 1 tbsp truffle oil or 1 tsp truffle shavings.

STUFFED TOMATOES

Serves 6

Preparation time: 15 minutes

Cooking time: 40 minutes

6 large tomatoes

200 g button mushrooms

2 onions

400 g pork (shoulder, spareribs)

400 g veal (chuck, neck)

1 bunch parsley

Salt

Pepper

Preheat the oven to 200°C - 400°F (gas mark 6). Cut off the tops of the tomatoes and remove their insides, setting this pulp aside. Wash the mushrooms and cut off their stems. Peel the onions. Cut the meat into large cubes.

Chop the meat with the onions and mushrooms using the food grinder with the fine plate on speed 2. Wash the parsley, then discard the stems. Add the leaves to the stuffing and season with salt and pepper. Fill the tomatoes with this mixture. Form the remaining stuffing into small balls. Place the stuffed tomatoes and stuffing balls in a baking dish.

Blend the reserved tomato pulp, season with salt and pepper, then add to the dish. Add the tomato tops and bake for 40 minutes.

VARIATIONS

You can replace the parsley with cilantro (coriander), the pork with lamb, and add ras el hanout spice mix to the stuffing. For a vegetarian version, replace the meat with bulgur or quinoa. You can also replace the tomatoes with round zucchini (courgettes).

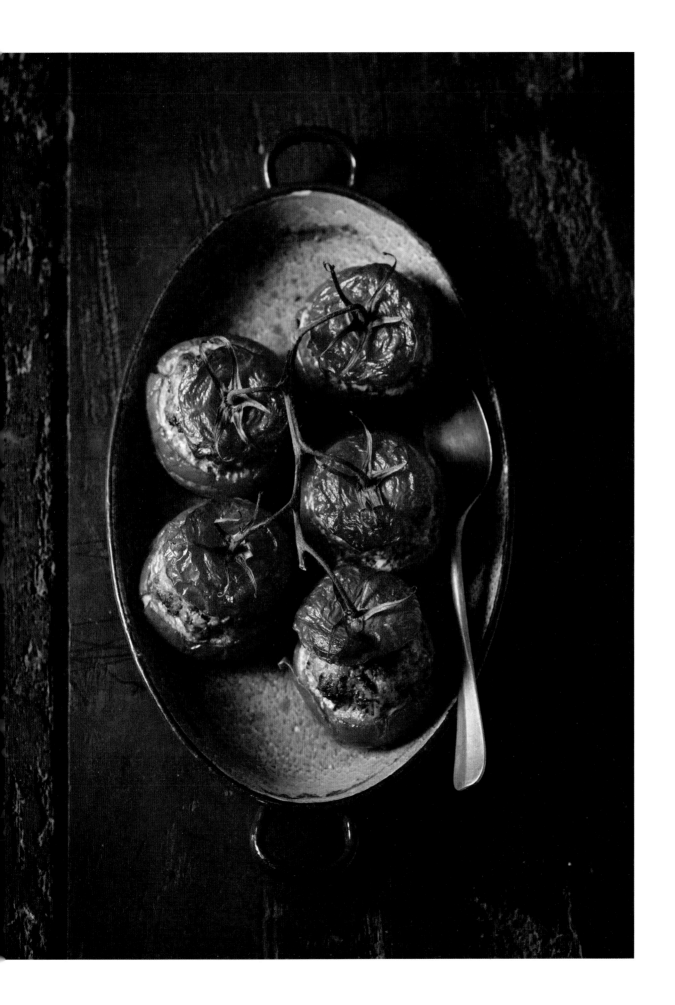

CHICKEN
SALAD
WITH LEMONGRASS

Serves 4

Preparation time: 20 minutes

Cooking time: 10 minutes

COOKING BROTH

In a saucepan, mix the lime juice, sugar, fish sauce, bouillon (stock) cube, and half a glass of water. Bring to a boil and let cook for 3 minutes over high heat while preparing the meat.

MEAT

Cut the chicken breasts into large cubes. Peel the garlic cloves and ginger. Cut the lemongrass into small pieces. Chop the chicken with the garlic cloves, ginger, and lemongrass using the food grinder with the coarse plate on speed 2. Drop the resulting preparation into the broth and let cook over medium heat for 5 minutes. Let cool.

VEGETABLES

Wash the cucumber, peel the onion, then cut into fine slices in the food processor attachment on speed 4 using the slicing disc set to the minimum size. Wash the lettuce and herbs and discard their stems. Coarsely chop the peanuts with a knife. Divide the rounds of cucumber and onion among 4 soup plates. Add a few lettuce leaves. Drain the chicken and add. Finally, add the herbs and peanuts. Drizzle with a few drops of lime juice and serve.

MEAT

400 g chicken breast

2 cloves garlic

5 cm fresh ginger root

1 stalk lemongrass

COOKING BROTH

Juice of 1 lime

1 tsp superfine (caster) sugar

2 tbsp Vietnamese fish sauce (nuoc mam)

1 chicken bouillon (stock) cube

VEGETABLES

1 cucumber

1 small red onion

1 head of lettuce

1 bunch cilantro (coriander)

1 bunch mint

50 g peanuts

Juice of 1/2 lime

TIPS

For a main course, add some rice or soy noodles. You can also add two shredded carrots and Thai basil.

STUFFED CHRISTMAS TURKEY

Serves 8

Preparation time: 20 minutes

Cooking time: 2 hours 30 minutes

1 (2.5-kg) turkey

2 onions

200 g pork (shoulder, spareribs)

200 g veal (chuck, neck)

100 g chicken livers

300 g porcini mushrooms (frozen)

500 g chestnuts (vacuum-packed, canned, or frozen)

1 egg

1/2 tsp quatre-épices spice blend

2 tbsp olive oil

Salt

Pepper

Remove the turkey from the refrigerator 1 hour before beginning to prepare the recipe so it will be at room temperature. Preheat the oven to 180°C - 350°F (gas mark 4).

Peel the onions and cut the meat into large pieces. Chop the meat with the onions, mushrooms, and 250 g of the chestnuts using the food grinder with the coarse plate on speed 2. Add the egg, spice blend, salt, and pepper, then mix. Stuff the turkey with this mixture, then truss. Brush the turkey with olive oil and season with salt and pepper. Place in a large roasting pan. Add 1 glass of water and bake.

After baking for 30 minutes, baste the turkey, then turn onto one side. After another 30 minutes, baste again, then turn onto the other side. After 30 minutes, set it flat again, baste, and add the remaining chestnuts to the pan. Cover the turkey with aluminum foil to keep the meat moist. Bake for another 1 hour.

When done, carve the turkey. Serve hot with the stuffing and chestnuts.

meat
& savory

For a more aromatic stuffing, you can add 1 tbsp brandy.
You can also add an apple to the stuffing, chopping it with the meat. This will give it a little sweetness and make it smoother.
For a gourmet version, add small cubes of foie gras to the stuffing.
To cook the turkey, modify the baking time according to its weight; allow about 1 hour per kilogram.

MASHED SWEET POTATOES
WITH HAM

Serves 4

Preparation time: 5 minutes

Cooking time: 15 minutes

600 g sweet potatoes

100 g cooked ham

100 ml cream

Salt

Pepper

Peel the sweet potatoes. Cut them into fine slices using the food processor attachment on speed 4 with the slicing disc set to the minimum size. Boil or steam for 10–15 minutes. Use the tip of a knife to check if they are cooked; it should pierce them with almost no resistance.

Chop the ham finely using a knife. Put the sweet potatoes into the bowl of the mixer fitted with the flat beater, then mix on speed 2. Gradually add the cream, salt, and pepper. When the sweet potato mash reaches the desired texture, add the ham, mix for another 30 seconds, then serve.

VARIATIONS

For an exotic version, replace the cream with coconut milk and add a pinch of quatre-épices spice mix or nutmeg. For children, replace the cream with Kiri® (light cream cheese).

BUCKWHEAT GALETTE MILLEFEUILLE
WITH CRAB

For 12 millefeuilles
(36 small crepes)

Preparation time: 10 minutes

Cooking time: 5 minutes

Resting time: 1 hour

FOR THE GALETTES

Put the flour and salt into the bowl of the mixer fitted with the wire whip. Turn on the mixer to speed 1. Add the egg and begin to gradually pour in the water. Next, pour in the milk and continue beating on speed 1 for 5–7 minutes. Let the batter rest for at least 1 hour.

Just before cooking the galettes, add the oil to the batter. Heat a small nonstick skillet or frying pan. When it is very hot, add a pat (knob) of butter, then pour in a little batter. After about 1 minute, flip it over and cook for another 30 seconds. Repeat until you have used all the batter. You'll get the job done faster if you use a few small skillets!

FOR THE FILLING

Make a vinaigrette: Chop the herbs and fresh ginger. Heat the oil, vinegar, and soy sauce in a small saucepan. When it comes to a boil, add the chopped herbs and ginger.
Heat the crabmeat with two-thirds of the vinaigrette.

Layer the millefeuille so that you have three small galettes and two layers of the crab-and-vinaigrette filling. Season to taste with the remaining vinaigrette.

GALETTES

250 g buckwheat flour

2 g salt

1 egg

500 g water

250 g milk

5 g neutral oil

Butter

FILLING

500 g crabmeat

3 sprigs cilantro (coriander)

3 sprigs parsley

¼ bunch chives

A little fresh ginger

25 g hazelnut oil

25 g walnut oil

1 tbsp balsamic vinegar

2 tbsp soy sauce

VARIATION & TIP

Use whatever herbs you have to hand; you can use dill, tarragon, etc. Serve with a salad of baby greens simply dressed with olive oil and balsamic vinegar.

ZUCCHINI AND SALMON GRATIN

Serves 4

Preparation time: 30 minutes

Cooking time: 45 minutes

800 g potatoes

2 kg zucchini (courgettes)

600 g salmon

2 cloves garlic

2 shallots

Olive oil

Bouquet garni

1 tbsp bread crumbs

2 tbsp Parmesan cheese

Peel the potatoes and cut into pieces. Wash the zucchini (courgettes) and cut into large pieces.
Peel the garlic and shallots and chop coarsely.
Brown the garlic, shallots, potatoes, and zucchini in a skillet or frying pan with a little olive oil for 15 minutes, stirring often. Let cool.
Puree all the ingredients using the fruit and vegetable strainer on speed 2. Set aside.
Cook the salmon with the bouquet garni in a large pot of boiling water for 8–10 minutes. Drain on paper towels, then flake using a fork.

Preheat the oven to 200°C - 400°F (gas mark 6).
Place the flaked salmon in a gratin dish and cover with the zucchini puree.
Sprinkle with bread crumbs and Parmesan and bake for 20 minutes until golden brown.

TIP

The zucchini can produce a lot of water when pureed using the fruit and vegetable strainer. If this occurs, let the whole mixture drain in a sieve. You can use the draining liquid to cook the salmon.

SCALLOP CARPACCIO
WITH GINGER AND LIME

Serves 6

Preparation time: 10 minutes

Resting time: 1 hour

300 g scallops, roe removed

2 limes

3 cm fresh ginger root

1 tbsp olive oil

1 pinch curry powder

Pink peppercorns

Salt

Pepper

Zest one of the limes and set the zest aside. Use the citrus juicer on speed 6 to juice the two limes. Pour the juice into a bowl. Peel the ginger and grate it finely using a grater. In a bowl, mix together the lime juice, ginger, olive oil, curry powder, salt, and pepper.

Use a sharp knife to cut the scallops into thin slices. Put into a large bowl and add the sauce, then mix. Cover with plastic wrap (clingfilm) and refrigerate for 1 hour.

Divide the scallops among 6 small plates, sprinkle with a little lime zest, and add a few pink peppercorns. Serve cold.

TIPS

Before cutting the scallops, make sure that the membrane that surrounds them has been completely removed. You can add chopped cilantro (coriander) and/or diced mango and avocado. You can also replace the curry powder with vanilla seeds.

SHRIMP PAD THAI

Serves 4

Preparation time: 30 minutes

Cooking time: 10 minutes

RICE NOODLES

225 g tapioca

225 g white basmati rice

TOPPING

250 g raw peeled shrimp (prawns)

2 eggs

2 tbsp peanut oil

1 shallot

2 cloves garlic

1 onion

2 tbsp nuoc mam sauce

3 tbsp soy sauce

1 tbsp brown sugar

100 g soybean sprouts

80 g unsalted peanuts

1/2 bunch cilantro (coriander)

1 lime

RICE NOODLES

Make rice flour as described on p. 30. Put 400 g flour into the bowl of the mixer fitted with the flex edge beater. Start the mixer on speed 2, then gradually add 400 ml boiling water. When the dough comes together, turn off the mixer, then roll the dough in the remaining flour. Cut the dough into 7–8 pieces. Flatten with a rolling pin and flour well.

Insert the pasta sheet roller into the hub of the mixer and set the thickness to 1. On speed 2, roll the dough several times, folding it over between each roll. Set the thickness to 2, then 3. Next, run the resulting dough through the fettuccine cutter attachment. Roll the pasta up into little nests and set on a floured towel.

TOPPING

Beat the eggs with a fork and cook them with 1 tbsp oil in a skillet frying pan for 2–3 minutes. Cut the scrambled egg into small pieces. Peel the shallot, garlic, and onion, then chop into cubes in the food processor attachment using the dicing disc on speed 6. Brown with 1 tbsp oil in the skillet for 5 minutes. Add the nuoc mam sauce, soy sauce, and brown sugar, then let caramelize for 2 minutes. Finally, add the shrimp (prawns), reduce the heat, and let cook for 5–6 minutes, stirring constantly.

Bring a pot of salted water to a boil. Drop in the rice noodles, a small amount at a time, and cook briefly for 1 minute. Drain with a slotted spoon and add to the skillet with the shrimp. Mix quickly. Remove from heat and add the scrambled egg, soybean sprouts, coarsely chopped peanuts, and cilantro (coriander) leaves. Serve with a slice of lime.

VARIATION

You can add julienned carrot to the pad Thai. You can also spice up this dish with chili pepper or Thai basil.

TUNA CEVICHE
WITH LIME AND CILANTRO

Preparation time: 10 minutes

Resting time: 1 hour

400 g fresh tuna

1 small red onion

1 small red bell pepper

1/2 bunch fresh cilantro (coriander)

2 limes

3 tbsp olive oil

Salt

Pepper

Cut the tuna into 2-cm cubes. Peel the onion. Cut the red bell pepper in half and remove its seeds. Cut into cubes in the food processor attachment using the dicing disc on speed 6.

In a large bowl, mix the tuna cubes with the onion and red bell pepper. Wash the cilantro (coriander) and discard the stems, then chop the leaves.

Zest 1 of the limes with a zester or fine grater. Use the citrus juicer on speed 6 to juice the limes. In a bowl, mix the lime juice and zest, olive oil, salt, and pepper. Pour over the fish, add the chopped cilantro (coriander), and mix. Cover with plastic wrap (clingfilm) and let marinate for 1 hour in the refrigerator. Serve cold.

VARIATIONS

You can also add diced mango or avocado to this recipe.
For a version with a little more kick, add a small chopped chili pepper or 1/2 tsp ground ginger.

CHEESE SOUFFLÉS

Serves 4

Preparation time: 25 minutes

Cooking time: 25–30 minutes

130 g Comté cheese

6 eggs

Butter + flour for the dishes

<u>**WHITE SAUCE**</u>

60 g butter

1 pinch salt

60 g type-55 flour

400 g low-fat (semi-skimmed) milk

1 pinch nutmeg

1 pinch Cayenne pepper

Shred the cheese finely using the Fresh Prep slicer/shredder with the medium shredding blade.
Separate the egg whites and yolks.
Lightly butter and flour the (straight-sided) soufflé dishes, being careful to shake off any extra flour.

WHITE SAUCE
Melt the butter in a saucepan over medium heat, then add the salt and flour. Whisk for 2 minutes, still over medium heat. Still whisking, gradually add the milk until the sauce begins to reach the proper sauce consistency. Add the nutmeg and pepper, then remove from heat.

FINISHING AND BAKING
Preheat the oven to 180°C - 350°F (gas mark 4) on the convection (fan-assisted) setting.
Add the shredded cheese and egg yolks to the white sauce and mix immediately.
Put the egg whites into the bowl of the mixer fitted with the wire whip, then start the mixer, raising the speed gradually to 10. Whip for about 1 minute 30 seconds, until the beaten whites hold stiff peaks.
Gently fold together the whites and white sauce, then divide among the soufflé dishes. Use your finger to level the top so that the edges will be clean. Bake for 25–30 minutes.

VARIATION

Soufflés can be adapted to fit your preferences—you can use whatever hard cheese you have in the refrigerator.

POTATO GRATIN
WITH ROQUEFORT CHEESE

Serves 4

Preparation time: 10 minutes

Cooking time: 40 minutes

800 g large potatoes

150 g Roquefort cheese

20 g butter

1 clove garlic

200 ml whipping cream

Salt

Pepper

Peel the potatoes, then cut them into thick strips using the vegetable sheet cutter on speed 2.

Butter a baking dish, then rub it with the garlic clove.
Place the potato strips into the dish.
Preheat the oven to 180 °C - 350°F (gas mark 4).

Pour the cream into a saucepan and heat. Add the crumbled Roquefort cheese and mix. Lightly season with salt and pepper, then pour the mixture over the potatoes. Bake for 35 minutes. Serve hot.

VARIATIONS

You can replace
the Roquefort with Comté
or Camembert cheese.
You can add button
mushrooms or minced leeks,
or even replace half
of the potatoes with squash.

CURLY FRIES
WITH PAPRIKA

Serves 4

Preparation time: 10 minutes

Cooking time: 5 minutes

800 g potatoes

1/2 tsp salt

1/2 tsp paprika

Oil for deep-frying

Peel the potatoes, then slice using the spiralizer with the medium spiral slice blade on speed 4. Pat dry with a clean cloth.

Heat the oil for deep-frying to 180°C - 350°F. Drop in the potato spirals and fry for 3–4 minutes. Watch closely, because the fries brown quickly. Drain on paper towels, then sprinkle with salt and paprika.

meat
& savory

VARIATION

You can make these fries with sweet potatoes.

ASPARAGUS, POACHED EGGS, AND WHIPPED CREAM

Serves 4

Preparation time: 30 minutes

Cooking time: 10-15 minutes

800 g green or white asparagus

200 ml cream

2 tbsp white vinegar

4 eggs

Zest of 1 orange

Salt

Pepper

Carefully peel the asparagus and trim off the ends. Steam or cook in a saucepan of salted boiling water for 8–10 minutes, according to their size. Drain. Blend two asparagus spears with 50 ml of the cream. Refrigerate.

Make the poached eggs: Bring a saucepan of boiling water to a boil with the vinegar. Crack an egg into a ramekin, then gently tip it into the boiling water. Using a slotted spoon, guide the white toward the yolk. Cook for 2–3 minutes, then retrieve the egg and drain it on of paper towels. Repeat with the other eggs.

Just before serving, pour the remaining cream into the bowl of the mixer fitted with the wire whip. Whip, gradually increasing the speed from 1 to 8, to make a good whipped cream. Gently fold in the reserved asparagus cream using a rubber spatula. Season with salt and pepper and grate the orange zest over the preparation. Mix gently.

Place the asparagus on the plates, add the poached eggs, then top with the whipped cream. Grind a little pepper on top, then serve.

VARIATIONS

You can add a little wasabi to give the whipped cream some kick.
You can sauté the asparagus in a skillet or frying pan with butter and 1 clove crushed garlic for a stronger flavor.

PASTA & GRAINS

CORN
MUFFINS

Makes 10 muffins

Preparation time: 15 minutes

Cooking time: 25 minutes

90 g corn kernels

120 g soft wheat

1 tsp baking powder

1 tsp baking soda

60 g sugar

2 large eggs

**100 ml low-fat
(semi-skimmed) milk**

2 tbsp honey

50 g butter

Oil for the muffin pan

Salt

Preheat the oven to 180°C - 350°F (gas mark 4).

Pour the corn and wheat into the grain mill set to the finest setting and start the mixer on speed 10. Transfer the resulting flour to the bowl of the mixer fitted with the flat beater. Add the baking powder, baking (bicarbonate of) soda, sugar, and a pinch of salt. Mix on speed 2 for 1 minute. Next, add the eggs and mix for 2 minutes.

Pour the milk and honey into a saucepan and add the butter. Heat the mixture, then add it to the bowl of the mixer and mix on speed 2 for 2 minutes.

Oil the cups of the muffin pan and pour in the batter. Bake for 25 minutes. Let cool, then remove the muffins from the pan. Serve for breakfast with butter and preserves.

VARIATION

For a gluten-free version, replace the wheat flour with flour made from 100 g whole-grain rice and 20 g cornstarch (cornflour).

GOURMET GRANOLA AND ALMOND MILK

Makes 1 large jar of granola and 800 ml almond milk

Preparation time: 15 minutes

Cooking time: 15 minutes

Resting time: Overnight

ALMOND MILK

100 g almonds

GOURMET GRANOLA

250 g rolled oats

50 g hazelnuts

50 g almonds

2 tbsp sunflower seeds

2 tbsp coconut oil

4 tbsp honey

1 pinch salt

100 g chocolate chips

ALMOND MILK
Make the almond milk as described on p. 40.

GOURMET GRANOLA
Preheat the oven to 150°C - 300°F (gas mark 2).
Grind the rolled oats in the grain mill set to the coarsest setting on speed 10.
Chop the hazelnuts and almonds with the Fresh Prep slicer/shredder fitted with the coarse shredding blade on speed 4.
In the bowl of the mixer fitted with the flat beater, combine the oats, chopped hazelnuts and almonds, sunflower seeds, and a pinch of salt.
In a small saucepan, melt the coconut oil with the honey.
Start the mixer on speed 2 and add the oil mixture. Mix for 2 minutes, then spread onto a baking sheet lined with parchment (baking) paper.
Bake for 15–20 minutes, mixing halfway through cooking. Keep a close eye on the granola during baking, because it browns quickly. Let cool; the granola will then harden. Finally, add the chocolate chips and mix.
Store in a sealed jar.

VARIATION

You can use a mixture of grain flakes (rice, quinoa, chestnut, buckwheat, etc.) Use different nuts and grains according to your preferences (macadamia nuts, pine nuts, pistachios, flaxseed, sesame seeds, etc.) You can also flavor the granola with vanilla or cinnamon. If you do not like the taste of coconut oil, replace it with walnut, hazelnut, or even grapeseed oil. You can also replace the honey with agave syrup or maple syrup.

HEALTHY PORRIDGE

Serves 2

Preparation time: 10 minutes

Cooking time: 5 minutes

50 g grain flakes (oats, quinoa, chestnut, rice, etc.)

200 ml milk

APPLE, HONEY, AND RAISIN PORRIDGE

1 apple

1 tbsp honey

1 tbsp raisins

PEAR AND CHOCOLATE PORRIDGE

1 bar dark chocolate

1 pear

COCONUT AND BANANA PORRIDGE

1 tbsp shredded coconut

1 banana

Pour the grain flakes into the grain mill set to a medium-fine setting and run the mixer on speed 10. Transfer the ground grains to a saucepan, add the milk, and cook for 5 minutes over medium heat, whisking constantly. Once the mixture thickens, add the topping (see below), then divide between 2 bowls. Serve immediately.

APPLE, HONEY, AND RAISIN PORRIDGE
Peel the apple, then cut into small cubes. Cook in a skillet or frying pan with 2 tbsp water for 10 minutes. Add the honey and cook another 5 minutes. Add the raisins just before serving.

PEAR AND CHOCOLATE PORRIDGE
Grate the chocolate with a grater and add to the porridge during cooking. Add a few cubes of fresh pear just before serving.

COCONUT AND BANANA PORRIDGE
Add the coconut to the porridge during cooking, then add the banana slices just before serving.

VARIATIONS

Use different grains to change the taste of the porridge. Add any nuts you like, and use different seasonal fresh fruit.

GLUTEN-FREE BREAD

Serves 12

Preparation time: 15 minutes

Cooking time: 40 minutes

Resting time: 1 hour
10 minutes

360 g brown rice

**180 g hulled buckwheat
or kasha**

180 g corn kernels

600 ml water

**2 tsp superfine (caster)
sugar**

**16 g gluten-free baker's
yeast**

2 pinches baking soda

10 g salt

Insert the grain mill into the hub of the mixer and set it to the finest setting. On speed 10, grind the brown rice, buckwheat, and corn into flour. This should produce 720 g flour; adjust the quantities, if necessary, to reach this weight.

Warm the water and pour into the bowl of the mixer. Add the sugar and yeast. Let stand for 10 minutes. The mixture should swell and become frothy. Next, add the flour, baking (bicarbonate of) soda, and salt. Mix with the dough hook on speed 4 for 2 minutes. Transfer the dough to a cake pan and let rise for 1 hour in a warm place.

Preheat the oven to 200°C - 400°F (gas mark 6). Bake for 40 minutes. After removing the bread from the oven, remove it from the pan and let cool. Let the bread cool completely before slicing.

TIPS & VARIATION

This bread is a little rustic, so don't be surprised.
Like all gluten-free breads, it should be eaten the day it is baked, because it turns stale quickly. You can slice and freeze it.
You can add 2 tsp guar gum to the dough; this will make the bread a little moister.
During baking, add a bowl of water to the oven to obtain a crunchier crust.
You can replace the buckwheat with the same amount of chickpeas by weight.

BUDDHA BOWL:
RICE PILAF AND VEGETABLES

Serves 4

Preparation time: 30 minutes

Cooking time: 1 hour

ROASTED CHICKPEAS
Preheat the oven to 180°C - 350°F (gas mark 4). Drain, rinse, and carefully dry the chickpeas. Put them onto a baking sheet lined with parchment paper. Drizzle with the olive oil, sprinkle with the cumin and salt, then mix with your hands to coat evenly. Bake for 30 minutes, stirring halfway through. Let cool; the chickpeas will become crunchy.

RICE PILAF
Add the rice to the grain mill set to the coarsest setting and run the mixer on speed 10. Set aside. Peel the onion, then cut into fine slices in the food processor attachment on speed 4 using the slicing disc set to the minimum size. Bring 600 ml of water to a boil with the bouillon (stock) cube. Brown the onion in a skillet or frying pan with the olive oil. When the onion is translucent, add the rice and mix until pearly white. Next, pour in all the hot bouillon immediately, then let cook for 25–30 minutes. Check to see if the rice is done, then keep warm.

VEGETABLES
Peel the carrots, then slice them in the food processor attachment using the julienne disc on speed 4. Cut the beets (beetroot) into small cubes. Peel the avocados and cut them into slices.

SAUCE
Mix all the ingredients to emulsify them.

ASSEMBLY
Place a little rice pilaf in four large bowls. Add some roasted chickpeas, sliced carrots, beets, and avocado. Drizzle the dressing over the vegetables and sprinkle with sunflower seeds. Serve immediately.

ROASTED CHICKPEAS

200 g chickpeas (canned or jarred)

1 tbsp olive oil

1 tsp ground cumin

Salt

RICE PILAF

200 g brown rice

1 onion

1 cube chicken bouillon

3 tbsp olive oil

Salt

VEGETABLES

2 carrots

2 beets (beetroot), cooked

2 avocados

2 tbsp sunflower seeds

SAUCE

3 tbsp olive oil

Juice of 1 lemon

Salt

Pepper

VARIATIONS & TIP

Use different grains—replace the rice with bulgur wheat, cracked corn, or quinoa.
Replace the sunflower seeds with toasted pumpkin or sesame seeds, pine nuts, etc. Use different seasonal vegetables.
You can also add some sweet potato dice roasted in coconut oil.

ALSATIAN TARTE FLAMBÉE— FLAMMEKUECHE

Serves 4

Preparation time: 15 minutes

Cooking time: 15 minutes

DOUGH

250 g type-45 flour

1 pinch salt

50 ml oil

150 ml warm water

TOPPING

2 onions

100 g fromage blanc or low-fat cream cheese

200 ml crème fraîche

200 g diced smoked bacon

Freshly ground pepper

Preheat the oven to 220°C - 425°F (gas mark 7).

Put the flour and salt into the bowl of the mixer fitted with the flex edge beater. Mix on speed 2, then add the oil and warm water and mix until the dough forms a ball. Flour and divide it into two equal halves. Use a rolling pin to roll them out on parchment (baking) paper to make two disks about 25 cm in diameter. Fold the edges in to make a slight border.

Peel the onions, then slice them in the food processor attachment set to the narrowest thickness at speed 2.

Mix the white cheese with the crème fraîche. Spread this mixture onto the dough and top with the onions and smoked bacon. Season generously with pepper.

Bake for 10 minutes, then place under the broiler (grill) for 5 minutes.

TIPS

You can also add some grated nutmeg. If you prefer a softer dough, make a pizza dough instead (see p. 34).

ASIAN-STYLE PORK RAVIOLI

Serves 4

Preparation time: 25 minutes

Cooking time: 20 minutes

Resting time: 1 hour

PASTA

400 g type-45 flour

Salt

FILLING

350 g pork

1 leek

2 cloves garlic

2 tbsp Vietnamese fish sauce (nuoc mam)

2 tbsp neutral oil

Salt

PASTA
Put the flour and a pinch of salt into the bowl of the mixer fitted with the flat beater. Mix on speed 2, adding warm water until the dough forms a ball. Replace the flat beater with the dough hook and knead on speed 4 for 3 minutes. Wrap the resulting dough in plastic wrap (clingfilm), then refrigerate for 30 minutes.

FILLING
Meanwhile, cut the meat into large cubes and peel the leek and garlic. Grind together in the food grinder with the fine plate on speed 4. Heat 1 tablespoon of olive oil in a skillet or frying pan and add the ground meat. Brown for 5 minutes, stirring constantly. Add the nuoc mam sauce, season lightly with salt, mix, and brown for another 5 minutes. Let cool completely.

RAVIOLI ASSEMBLY AND COOKING
Insert the pasta sheet roller into the hub of the mixer and set the thickness to 1. On speed 2, make the dough more pliable by rolling it several times, folding it over between each roll. Next, turn the thickness to 2, then reduce it incrementally to 4, making sure to flour the dough well to keep it from sticking. Make several long sheets 15 cm wide, trimming the edges to make them even.

Attach the ravioli maker. Fold the dough in half and pinch it between the rollers. Attach the hopper and distribute a little filling along the length of the pasta sheet, breaking up any lumps. Use all the dough to make ravioli. Let dry for 10 minutes, then separate and place on a floured surface.

Bring a large pot of water to a boil and cook the ravioli for 5 minutes. Heat 1 tablespoon of olive oil in a skillet or frying pan and brown the ravioli. Serve with rice and soy sauce.

TIPS

To help your ravioli turn out well, let the filling cool completely before starting the filling process.
You can add a little ginger to the filling for flavor.

SPINACH
AND RICOTTA
RAVIOLI

Serves 4

Preparation time: 30 minutes

Cooking time: 20 minutes

Resting time: 30 minutes

PASTA

200 g type-45 flour

200 g semolina

4 eggs

FILLING

400 g frozen spinach

2 cloves garlic

100 g shelled walnuts

100 g ricotta cheese

Salt

Pepper

Make the pasta as described on p. 33, then refrigerate for 30 minutes.

FILLING
Cook the spinach from frozen in boiling water for 10 minutes. Drain, then squeeze to remove as much cooking water as possible. Peel the garlic. Grind the spinach, walnuts, and garlic in the food grinder with the fine plate on speed 4. Transfer to the bowl of the mixer fitted with the flex edge beater, add the ricotta, salt, and pepper, and mix on speed 4 for 2 minutes. Store in the refrigerator; the mixture should be cold when you prepare the ravioli.

Insert the pasta sheet roller into the hub of the mixer and set the thickness to 1. On speed 2, make the dough more pliable by rolling it several times, folding it over between each roll. Next, reduce the thickness to 2, then reduce it incrementally to 4, making sure to flour the dough well to keep it from sticking. Make several long sheets 15 cm wide, trimming the edges to make them even.

Attach the ravioli maker. Fold the dough in half and pinch it between the rollers. Attach the hopper and distribute a little filling along the length of the pasta sheet. Use all the dough to make ravioli. Let dry for 10 minutes, then separate and place on a floured surface.

Bring a large pot of water to a boil and cook the ravioli for 5 minutes. Serve with a drizzle of good olive oil.

TIPS

You can add a pinch of nutmeg to the filling and replace the walnuts with pine nuts. You can also add 50 g of cured ham and grind it with the spinach.

CANNELLONI

Serves 6

Preparation time: 20 minutes

Cooking time: 45 minutes

Resting time: 30 minutes

100 g grated Parmesan cheese

PASTA

200 g type-45 flour

2 eggs

1/2 tsp salt

STUFFING

1 onion

1 clove garlic

1 tbsp olive oil

150 g frozen leaf spinach

150 g button mushrooms

1/2 bunch basil

1 egg

200 g ricotta cheese

Salt

WHITE SAUCE

25 g butter

3 tbsp flour

700 ml milk

Salt

Pepper

PASTA

Make the pasta as described on p. 33 using the ingredients listed here, then refrigerate for 30 minutes. Insert the pasta sheet roller into the hub of the mixer and set the thickness to 1. On speed 2, make the dough more pliable by rolling it several times, folding it over between each roll. Next, set the thickness to 2, then increase it incrementally to 5, making sure to flour the dough well to prevent it from sticking. Set on a work surface and cut out rectangles about 10 cm long. Let dry on a floured towel while preparing the stuffing.

STUFFING

Peel the onion and garlic, chop them coarsely, then brown them in a sauté pan with the olive oil. Cut the mushrooms in half, then add along with the spinach. Brown for 10 minutes. Transfer the stuffing to the bowl of the mixer, add the basil leaves, egg, ricotta cheese, and salt, then stir together.

WHITE SAUCE

In a saucepan, melt the butter, then whisk in the flour. Still whisking, gradually add the milk until the mixture begins to thicken. Add salt and pepper. Pour half the white sauce into the bottom of a baking dish.

Preheat the oven to 200°C - 400°F (gas mark 6). Bring a large pot of salted water to a boil. Drop in the sheets of pasta, two at a time, and cook for 3 minutes, making sure they do not stick to one another. Drain, then lay flat. Put a little stuffing along one edge, then roll up. Gently place them on top of the white sauce in the baking dish. Cover with white sauce, sprinkle with Parmesan cheese, then bake for 35 minutes. Serve hot.

VARIATIONS

You can replace the white sauce with a good tomato sauce. You can also add some small cured ham dice to the stuffing.
To flavor the white sauce, add a dash of grated nutmeg.

SPAGHETTI ALLA PASSATA

Serves 4

Preparation time: 15 minutes

Cooking time: 15–20 minutes

PASTA
Make the dough as described on p. 33, then make the spaghetti using the pasta sheet roller, then the spaghetti cutter attachment. Set on a floured towel or the pasta drying rack.

PASSATA
Make the passata as described on p. 31.

Cook the pasta in a large pot of boiling water for 4–5 minutes. Drain, then serve with the hot passata, chopped basil, and Parmesan cheese shavings.

PASTA

120 g type-45 flour

120 g whole-wheat (wholemeal) flour

160 g semolina

4 eggs

½ tsp salt

PASSATA

1 kg tomatoes

2 tbsp olive oil

Salt

TOPPING

1 small bunch basil

50 g Parmesan cheese shavings

TIP

You can add a red bell pepper and a clove of garlic to the tomato sauce to give it more flavor.

SPAGHETTI CARBONARA

Serves 4

Preparation time: 20 minutes

Cooking time: 10 minutes

PASTA

200 g type-45 flour

200 g semolina

4 eggs

1/2 tsp salt

TOPPING

200 g smoked bacon

4 tbsp crème fraîche

120 g grated Parmesan cheese

4 egg yolks

Pepper

Make the pasta dough as described on p. 33 and divide it into small pieces. Run through the gourmet pasta press fitted with the spaghetti disc on speed 10 to make pasta about 24 cm long. Set on a floured towel.

Bring a large pot of salted water to a boil. Drop in the spaghetti and cook for about 5 minutes. Make sure to reserve 1 ladleful of the cooking water.

In a bowl, mix together the crème fraîche, grated Parmesan cheese, egg yolks, and pepper. Brown the bacon in a large, deep skillet or frying pan. Once the bacon is brown, add the drained pasta, then pour in the egg mixture. Mix and continue to cook for 2 minutes. Add a little hot cooking water to bring the mix together. Serve hot.

TIP

You can add a pinch of nutmeg.

L A S A G N E

Serves 6

Preparation time: 30 minutes

Cooking time: 1 hour
10 minutes

Resting time: 30 minutes

150 g Parmesan cheese

PASTA

200 g type-45 flour

2 eggs

1/2 tsp salt

BOLOGNESE SAUCE

400 g ground beef

2 onions

1 clove garlic

1 tbsp olive oil

2 carrots

500 g diced tomatoes

Salt

Pepper

WHITE SAUCE

25 g butter

3 tbsp flour

700 ml milk

PASTA
Make the dough as described on p. 33 using the ingredients listed here, then refrigerate for 30 minutes. Insert the pasta sheet roller into the hub of the mixer and set the thickness to 1. On speed 2, make the dough more pliable by rolling it several times, folding it over between each roll. Next, turn the thickness to 2, then reduce it incrementally to 5, making sure to flour the dough well to prevent it from sticking. Transfer to the work surface and cut out rectangles the same size as your baking dish. Let dry under a floured cloth while you prepare the sauce.

BOLOGNESE SAUCE
Peel the onions and garlic and chop finely. Brown them with the olive oil in a deep skillet or frying pan. Peel the carrots and cut into small cubes. Add them along with the meat, tomatoes, salt, and pepper. Let simmer for 15 minutes.

WHITE SAUCE
In a saucepan, melt the butter, then use a whisk to beat in the flour by hand. Still whisking, gradually add the milk until the mixture begins to thicken. Season with salt and pepper.

Preheat the oven to 200°C - 400°F (gas mark 6). Bring a large pot of salted water to a boil. Drop in the lasagna two at a time, cooking for 3 minutes, making sure that they do not stick to one another. Drain, then lay flat.

Place a layer of pasta in the bottom of a baking dish, then cover with the Ragú sauce, white sauce, and then Parmesan cheese. Repeat until all ingredients have been used, finishing with a layer of pasta covered with white sauce and Parmesan cheese.
Bake for 40 minutes. Serve hot.

TIPS
You can add mushrooms or other vegetables to the Bolognese sauce. You can grind the meat, carrots, onions, and garlic yourself using the food grinder with the coarse plate.

VEGETARIAN SWEET POTATO LASAGNE WITH FRESH GOAT CHEESE

Serves 6

Preparation time: 30 minutes

Cooking time: 1 hour 10 minutes

VEGETABLE LASAGNE

2 large sweet potatoes

50 g grated Pecorino cheese

VEGETABLE BOLOGNESE SAUCE

400 g organic pumpkin

300 g carrots

2 onions

2 cloves garlic

1 tbsp olive oil

400 g tomato coulis

1 tbsp herbes de Provence

Salt

Pepper

WHITE SAUCE WITH FRESH GOAT CHEESE

25 g butter

3 tbsp type-45 flour

500 ml low-fat (semi-skimmed) milk

200 g fresh goat cheese

Salt

Pepper

VEGETABLE BOLOGNESE SAUCE
Wash the pumpkin and peel the carrots, onions, and garlic cloves, then chop into cubes in the food processor attachment using the dicing disc on speed 6. Brown them with the olive oil in a large skillet or frying pan. Add the tomato coulis, herbes de Provence, and salt and pepper. Mix, then let simmer for 30 minutes over low heat.

WHITE SAUCE WITH FRESH GOAT CHEESE
In a saucepan, melt the butter, then whisk in the flour. Still whisking, gradually add the milk until the mixture begins to thicken. Crumble the fresh goat cheese and add, whisking it in thoroughly. Season with salt and pepper and set aside.

VEGETABLE LASAGNE
Peel the sweet potatoes, then cut into thick slices using the vegetable sheet cutter on speed 4.

ASSEMBLY
Preheat the oven to 180°C - 350°F (gas mark 4).

Place a layer of sweet potato slices in the bottom of a baking dish and cover with the vegetable Bolognese sauce, then with white sauce. Repeat until all the ingredients are used up, ending with a layer of sweet potato slices covered with white sauce and sprinkled with grated Pecorino cheese. Bake for 40 minutes. Serve hot.

TIPS

For an exotic version, replace half the pumpkin with red lentils, the herbes de Provence with curry powder, and make the white sauce with coconut milk. For a gluten-free version, make the white sauce with rice flour.

PESTO TAGLIATELLI

Serves 4

Preparation time: 15 minutes

Cooking time: 5 minutes

PASTA

240 g type-45 flour

160 g semolina

4 eggs

1/2 tsp salt

PESTO

50 g basil

2 cloves garlic

50 g pine nuts

50 g Parmesan cheese

80 ml olive oil

Salt

PASTA
Make the dough as described on p. 33, then make the tagliatelli using the pasta sheet roller and cutter. Set on a floured towel or the pasta drying rack.

PESTO
Make the pesto as described on p. 31.

Cook the pasta in a large pot of salted water for 4–5 minutes. Serve with the pesto.

BUCATINI
ALL'AMATRICIANA

Serves 4

Preparation time: 15 minutes

Cooking time: 25 minutes

Resting time: 30 minutes

PASTA

200 g type-45 flour

200 g semolina

4 eggs

1/2 tsp salt

SAUCE

1 kg tomatoes

2 onions

1 clove garlic

150 g bacon

1 tbsp olive oil

1 cup white wine

1 small whole chili pepper (adjust to taste)

20 g grated Pecorino cheese

Salt

PASTA

Make the dough (see p. 33) and divide it into small pieces. Run through the gourmet pasta press fitted with the bucatini disc on speed 10 to make pasta about 24 cm long. Set on a floured towel.

SAUCE

Wash the tomatoes, peel the onions and garlic clove, then cut into quarters. Puree into a coulis using the fruit and vegetable strainer.

Cut the bacon into fine slices, then put into a skillet or frying pan with the olive oil. Let brown for 2 minutes, stirring constantly. Pour in a little wine and let it reduce. Add the tomato coulis, the rest of the wine, and the salt and chili pepper, then simmer over low heat for 20 minutes.

Bring a large pot of salted water to a boil. Drop in the bucatini and cook for about 5 minutes. Drain, add to the pan with the sauce, then mix. Remove from heat, add the grated Pecorino cheese, and serve.

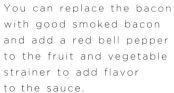

TIP & VARIATION

You can replace the bacon with good smoked bacon and add a red bell pepper to the fruit and vegetable strainer to add flavor to the sauce.

FUSILLI ALLA BURRATA WITH SHRIMP

Serves 4

Preparation time: 15 minutes

Cooking time: 20 minutes

Make the dough as described on p. 33 and divide into small pieces. Run through the gourmet pasta press fitted with the fusilli disc on speed 3 to make pasta about 4 cm long. Set on a floured towel.

Defrost the shrimp (prawns). Peel the carrots, celery root (celeriac), onion, and garlic cloves, then chop into cubes in the food processor attachment using the dicing disc on speed 6.

Brown the vegetables with the olive oil in a deep skillet or frying pan for 3 minutes. Quarter the cherry tomatoes and add them along with the shrimp. Add water to cover. Cook until the vegetables are just tender.

Wash the basil and discard the stems, then chop the leaves. Cook the fusilli in a large pot of salted boiling water for 5 minutes. Add them to the sauce with the basil and mix. Remove from heat, then cut the burrata into small pieces and add. Serve immediately.

PASTA

200 g type-45 flour

200 g semolina

4 eggs

1/2 tsp salt

SAUCE

300 g peeled shrimp (prawns), frozen

1 carrot

20 g celery root (celeriac)

1 onion

2 cloves garlic

2 tbsp olive oil

12 cherry tomatoes

1 bunch basil

180 g burrata

Salt

Pepper

22
4

MACARONI
WITH PORCINI
AND THYME

Serves 4

Preparation time: 15 minutes

Cooking time: 15 minutes

PASTA

200 g type-45 flour

200 g semolina

4 eggs

1/2 tsp salt

TOPPING

1 shallot

250 porcini (cep) mushrooms

1 tbsp extra-virgin olive oil

1 sprig fresh thyme

Black pepper

50 g Parmesan cheese

Make the dough as described on p. 33 and divide into small pieces. Run through the gourmet pasta press fitted with the large macaroni disc on speed 6 to make pasta about 5 cm long. Set on a floured towel.

Peel and chop the shallot. Trim off the mushroom stems, then wash them gently with paper towels. Mince. In a deep skillet or frying pan, cook the shallot with olive oil without letting it brown. Add the mushrooms and thyme and cook until they just begin to brown.

Bring a large pot of salted water to a boil. Drop in the macaroni and cook for about 5 minutes. Drain, then add them to the skillet along with a little cooking water and mix. Remove from heat, add the grated Parmesan cheese, season with pepper, and serve.

TIPS & VARIATIONS

You can use frozen mushrooms.
For a main course, you can serve this pasta dish with thin slices of cured Italian ham.
You can replace the thyme with parsley.
For a more rustic flavor, replace half of the type-45 flour with whole-wheat flour.

MINI MACARONI & CHEESE

Serves 4

Preparation time: 15 minutes

Cooking time: 40 minutes

Resting time: 30 minutes

PASTA

150 g type-45 flour

150 g semolina

3 eggs

1/2 tsp salt

CHEDDAR SAUCE

25 g butter

3 tbsp flour

700 ml milk

100 g shredded cheddar + 50 g for baking

A pinch of nutmeg

Salt

Pepper

Preheat the oven to 180°C - 350°F (gas mark 4). Make the dough (see p. 33) and divide into small pieces. Run through the gourmet pasta press fitted with the small macaroni disc on speed 6 to make pasta about 4 cm long. Set on a floured towel.

In a saucepan, melt the butter, then use a whisk to beat in the flour. Still whisking, gradually add the milk until the mixture begins to thicken. Finally, add the shredded cheddar, nutmeg, salt, and pepper.

Bring a large pot of salted water to a boil. Drop in the mini macaroni and cook for about 5 minutes. Add the cheddar sauce and mix. Transfer this mixture to a baking dish. Add the rest of the cheddar and bake for 30 minutes. Serve very hot.

TIPS

You can add bread crumbs on top of the macaroni and cheese for a little added crunch. Serve with a green salad.

CHEESE AND PEPPER
RIGATONI

Serves 4

Preparation time: 15 minutes

Cooking time: 5 minutes

PASTA

200 g type-45 flour

200 g semolina

4 eggs

1/2 tsp salt

CHEESE-PEPPER SAUCE

40 g grated Pecorino cheese

80 g grated Parmesan cheese

8 g ground pepper

20 g olive oil

GARNISH

A few flakes Parmesan cheese

PASTA
Make the dough as described on p. 33 and divide it into small pieces. Run through the gourmet pasta press fitted with the rigatoni disc on speed 6 to make pasta about 4 cm long. Set on a floured towel.

Bring a large pot of salted water to a boil. Drop in the rigatoni and cook for about 5 minutes.

CHEESE-PEPPER SAUCE
Put the Pecorino and Parmesan cheeses, pepper, and olive oil into a bowl. Add a little of the pasta cooking water and mix until just smooth.

Drain the pasta and place in a large serving dish. Pour the sauce over the pasta and mix gently to coat the pasta thoroughly with the sauce. Add a few flakes of Parmesan cheese and serve.

TIP

For children's sensitive palates, replace the pepper with a little dried oregano.

PUMPKIN GNOCCHI WITH SAGE BUTTER

Serves 4

Preparation time: 20 minutes

Cooking time: 35 minutes

PARMESAN CHEESE GNOCCHI

200 g potatoes

300 g pumpkin

1 egg yolk

250 g type-45 flour

A pinch of grated nutmeg

Salt

SAGE BUTTER

50 g butter

8 sage leaves

Salt

Pepper

FINISHING

Grated Parmesan

Peel the potatoes and wash the pumpkin. Cut into cubes and steam for 20–30 minutes. Put into the bowl of the mixer fitted with the flex edge beater and mix on speed 2 for 2 minutes. Add the egg yolk. Next, add the flour, salt, and nutmeg, a little at a time, mixing for 2 minutes.

Flour your work surface and the dough. Roll the dough into ropes 1–2 cm in diameter, and cut into pieces 3–4 cm long. Roll over the back of a fork or a gnocchi board.

Bring a large pot of salted water to a boil, then drop in the gnocchi and cook for a few minutes. They are cooked when they rise to the surface. Drain the gnocchi.

Melt the butter in a skillet or frying pan with the sage leaves. Add the drained gnocchi, rolling them in the sage butter. Season with salt and pepper, and serve with Parmesan cheese.

VARIATIONS & TIP

You can replace the pumpkin with a different winter squash. Add a crushed garlic clove to the sage butter. If your puree is too wet, you can dry it out for a few minutes in a saucepan.

SWEETS

APRICOT
AND PISTACHIO
CREAM TART

Serves 6

Preparation time: 15 minutes

Cooking time: 50 minutes

Resting time: 1 hour

SWEET PASTRY
Make the dough as described on p. 36 and refrigerate for 1 hour.

Preheat the oven to 180°C - 350°F (gas mark 4). Butter and flour a 28-cm-diameter tart pan. Roll out the dough on a floured work surface and use to line the tart pan. Prick the dough with a fork, cover with parchment (baking) paper and weights (either pie weights or dried beans), and blind bake for 10 minutes.

FILLING
While the pastry is cooking, mix the eggs, melted butter, sugar, almond meal (ground almonds), and pistachio paste in the bowl of the mixer fitted with the flex edge beater on speed 2 for 2 minutes.

Cut the apricots in half and remove their pits (stones). Coarsely chop the pistachios with a knife. When the pastry is baked, fill it with the pistachio cream, then arrange the apricots on top. Sprinkle with vanilla sugar and chopped pistachios. Bake for 40 minutes. Let cool before serving.

SWEET PASTRY

100 g butter

70 g confectioner's (icing) sugar

1 pinch salt

35 g egg

175 g type-45 flour

30 g almond meal (ground almonds)

FILLING

2 eggs

80 g butter, melted

60 g sugar

80 g almond meal (ground almonds)

20 g pistachio paste

12 apricots

50 g unsalted pistachios

11 g vanilla sugar

TIPS

If you do not have any pistachio paste, blend 20 g unsalted pistachios as finely as possible.
During the winter, you can make this tart with pears.

BANANA-CARAMEL (BANOFFEE) PIE

Makes 1 22-cm pie

Preparation time: 30 minutes

Cooking time: 3 hours
15 minutes

Resting time: 1 hour

CARAMEL

1 can sweetened condensed milk (400 g)

SWEET PASTRY

100 g butter

80 g confectioners' (icing) sugar

1 egg

200 g type-45 flour

40 g almond meal (ground almonds)

Salt

TOPPING

300 ml whipping cream, very cold

30–40 g confectioners' (icing) sugar

3 bananas

Cocoa powder

CARAMEL
Put the can of sweetened condensed milk into a saucepan deep enough to submerge the can and add water to cover. Bring to a boil and simmer for 3 hours, adding water as necessary. Cool under cold running water.

SWEET PASTRY
Put the softened butter and confectioners' (icing) sugar into the bowl of a stand mixer fitted with the flat beater. Mix on speed 2 for 2 minutes. Add the egg and mix for 1 minute. Add the flour, almond meal (ground almonds), and salt and mix until the dough comes together. Wrap in plastic wrap (clingfilm) and refrigerate for 1 hour.

Preheat the oven to 180°C - 350°F (gas mark 4). Roll out the dough using a rolling pin and use it to line a buttered 22-cm pie plate. Blind bake for 15 minutes. Let cool.

TOPPING
Put the cold whipping cream into the bowl of the mixer fitted with the wire whip. Whip, starting on speed 1 and gradually increasing the speed to 8. When the cream begins to whip up, add the confectioners' sugar and continue to beat until stiff peaks form.

Spread the caramel over the bottom of the pastry shell (case). Peel the bananas, cut them into rounds, and distribute them over the top. Cover generously with whipped cream and sprinkle with cocoa powder.

If you are short on time, you can buy prepared caramel. You can make a delicious ice cream with the leftover caramel (see p. 314).
The bananas should not be exposed to the air, so cover them with whipped cream immediately.
You can flavor the pastry with cinnamon or a quatre-épices spice blend.

APPLE ROSE TART

Serves 8

Preparation time: 30 minutes

Cooking time: 1 hour

Resting time: 30 minutes

SHORTBREAD PASTRY

250 g type-45 flour

40 g superfine (caster) sugar

3 pinches salt

125 g butter

1 egg

FILLING

5 apples

2 tbsp superfine (caster) sugar

TOPPING

1 kg tart apples

4 tbsp brown sugar

SHORTBREAD PASTRY
Make the pastry as described on p. 36, then refrigerate for 30 minutes.

FILLING
Peel and quarter the apples, then cut them into cubes in the food processor attachment using the dicing disc on speed 6. Put into a saucepan with the sugar and 2 tablespoons of water. Let soften over low heat, stirring often, for 20 minutes. Cool.

ASSEMBLY AND FINISHING
Preheat the oven to 180°C - 350°F (gas mark 4) on the convection (fan-assisted) setting.

Roll out the dough on a floured work surface using a rolling pin. Butter a tart pan and line it with the dough disk. Spread the filling over the bottom of the tart.

Wash the apples, but do not peel. Slice the first apple using the vegetable sheet cutter. Place the resulting apple strip on a plate and microwave at maximum power for 2 minutes. This will soften the strip to make it more workable. Cut a few small 10-cm strips and curl them into rolls. Cut each in half to create two rosettes. Arrange them on top of the filling. Repeat until the tart is covered with rosettes.

Sprinkle with brown sugar and bake for 40 minutes. Serve warm with whipped cream or vanilla ice cream.

VARIATIONS

You can replace the filling with pastry cream, flavoring it with vanilla, cinnamon, or orange flower water. You can also choose to make one large rose by rolling the apple strips into a spiral.

LEMON MERINGUE PIE

Makes 1 20-cm pie

Preparation time: 1 hour

Cooking time: 15–20 minutes

Resting time: 2 hours
30 minutes

SHORTBREAD PASTRY
Prepare the shortbread pastry as described on p. 36 and refrigerate for 30 minutes. Use to line the pie plate. Preheat the oven to 180°C - 350°F (gas mark 4) and bake the pie shell for 15–20 minutes.

LEMON FILLING
Make a lemon curd as described on p. 41. Refrigerate for 2 hours.

ITALIAN MERINGUE
Make an Italian meringue as described on p. 42 and let cool.

GARNISH
Use a pastry bag to pipe the meringue decoratively over the surface of the pie. Brown lightly with a chef's blowtorch. Zest the lime using a Microplane® zester. Add a few basil leaves, if desired.

SHORTBREAD PASTRY

250 g type-45 flour

125 g sugar

125 g butter

1 egg

Salt

LEMON FILLING

120 g lemon juice

Zest of 1 lemon

110 g eggs

100 g superfine (caster) sugar

150 g butter

ITALIAN MERINGUE

225 g meringue (see p. 42)

GARNISH

Zest of 1 lime

Confectioners' (icing) sugar

Basil leaves (optional)

VARIATION

You can also make a lemon-basil cream. For this, remove the leaves from a dozen sprigs of basil, cook them in the lemon cream, and blend the whole mixture.

CHOCOLATE-CARAMEL TART

Serves 6

Preparation time: 20 minutes

Cooking time: 25 minutes

Resting time: 1 hour
30 minutes

SWEET PASTRY
Make the dough as described on p. 36 and refrigerate for 1 hour.

Preheat the oven to 180°C - 350°F (gas mark 4). Butter and flour a 28-cm-diameter tart pan. Roll out the dough on a floured work surface and use to line the tart pan. Prick the dough with a fork, cover with parchment (baking) paper and weights (either pie weights or dried beans), and blind bake for 20 minutes. Remove the paper and the weights and bake for another 5 minutes. Once baked, let cool.

CARAMEL
Put the sugar and 1 tbsp of water into a saucepan and make a caramel. Whisk in the cream, making sure that it does not burn. Finally, add the butter, mix, then pour into the tart shell (case). Let cool for 30 minutes in the refrigerator.

CHOCOLATE GANACHE
Make the ganache as described on p. 41. Use to fill the tart shell (case).

SWEET PASTRY

100 g butter

70 g confectioner's (icing) sugar

1 pinch salt

35 g egg

175 g type-45 flour

30 g almond meal (ground almonds)

CARAMEL

250 g sugar

150 ml cream

100 g lightly salted butter

CHOCOLATE GANACHE

200 g dark chocolate

150 ml cream

20 g butter

VARIATIONS

You can add some crushed nuts to the caramel: hazelnuts, almonds, peanuts. You can also sprinkle the tart with sesame seeds.

RICOTTA AND PINE NUT TART

Serves 8

Preparation time: 40 minutes

Cooking time: 40 minutes

Resting time: 30 minutes

SWEET PASTRY

Put the softened butter, sugar, and almond meal (ground almonds) into the bowl of the mixer fitted with the flex edge beater and mix on speed 2 for 3 minutes. Add the egg, then the flour. Beat until the dough just comes together into a ball. Wrap in plastic wrap (clingfilm) and refrigerate for 30 minutes.

Preheat the oven to 180°C - 350°F (gas mark 4). Roll out the dough on a floured work surface and use to line a 25-cm-diameter tart pan. Prick the dough with a fork and blind bake for 10 minutes.

FILLING

Put the ricotta cheese, crème fraîche, egg yolks, sugar, lemon juice, and lemon zest into the bowl of the mixer fitted with the wire whip. Mix on speed 2 for 3 minutes. On speed 1, add the pine nuts and mix for 30 seconds. Pour the filling into the tart shell (case).

Bake for 30 minutes. The pastry should be golden brown and the filling firm to the touch. Let cool completely.

SWEET PASTRY

150 g butter, softened

100 g confectioners' (icing) sugar

50 g almond meal (ground almonds)

1 egg, beaten

250 g type-45 flour

FILLING

350 g ricotta cheese

1 tbsp crème fraîche

3 egg yolks

100 g sugar

Juice and zest of 1 lemon

100 g pine nuts

TIPS

If you have leftover dough, you can make little cookies. Replace the lemon juice and zest with orange juice and zest.

FRENCH PEAR TART

Makes 1 26-cm tart

Preparation time: 30 minutes

Cooking time: 40 minutes

Resting time: 1 hour

3 ripe pears

30 g sliced (flaked) almonds

SWEET PASTRY

100 g butter

80 g confectioners' (icing) sugar

1 egg

200 g type-45 flour

40 g almond meal (ground almonds)

Salt

FRANGIPANE

60 g butter

1 pinch salt

1/2 tsp vanilla powder

40 g sugar

1 small egg

65 g almond meal (ground almonds)

5 g flour

50 g rum

SWEET PASTRY
Make the sweet pastry dough as described on p. 36, then refrigerate for 1 hour.

FRANGIPANE
Soften the butter, then put it into the bowl of the mixer fitted with the flex edge beater. Start the mixer on speed 1. Add the salt, vanilla, and sugar. Mix for about 1 minute, then add the egg. Once the egg is thoroughly incorporated, add the almond meal (ground almonds), flour, and rum.

Peel the pears, cut them in half, and remove the stem with the tip of a knife.
Cut the pear halves into slices, being careful to preserve their shape.

Preheat the oven to 170°C - 340°F (gas mark 3–4) on the convection (fan-assisted) setting. Butter the tart pan.
Roll out the sweet dough to a thickness of about 3 mm and prick. Flip over and use to line the tart pan. Trim off any extra dough using a small knife.
Spread the frangipane over the tart shell (case), then gently place the pear slices on top, their tops pointing outward.
Sprinkle the spaces between the pears with slivered (flaked) almonds.

Bake for about 40 minutes.

TIPS

To save time, you do not have to cut the pears into slices. In summer, you can make a good version of this recipe with ripe peaches. They pair well with the frangipane.

APPLE & PEAR CRISP

Serves 4–6

Preparation time: 10 minutes

Cooking time: 30 minutes

5 apples

3 pears

150 g type-45 flour

125 g almond meal (ground almonds)

150 g brown sugar

200 g salted butter

1 tsp vanilla powder

Preheat the oven to 180°C - 350°F (gas mark 4).

Peel the fruits and slice them in the food processor attachment on speed 1 using the slicing disc set to the minimum size. Grease and sugar a baking dish about 20 x 30 cm in size and spread the fruit slices over the bottom.

In the bowl of the mixer fitted with the flat beater, mix the flour, almond meal (ground almonds), brown sugar, salted butter, and vanilla powder on speed 4 for 2 minutes. Cover the fruits with the resulting dough, crumbling it with your fingertips. Bake for 30 minutes. Serve warm or cold with cream or vanilla ice cream.

VARIATIONS

Replace the almond meal with hazelnut flour (ground hazelnuts) and add some chopped hazelnuts.
You can also add spices: cinnamon, ginger, tonka bean, etc.
Use different fruits, depending on the season.

CARROT CAKE

Serves 6

Preparation time: 20 minutes

Cooking time: 1 hour

CARROT CAKE

300 g carrots

260 g type-45 flour

190 g brown sugar

11 g baking powder

1/2 tsp cinnamon

1/2 tsp nutmeg

1/2 tsp ground ginger

1 tsp vanilla extract

3 eggs

250 ml sunflower oil

FROSTING (ICING)

50 g butter, softened

150 g cream cheese

150 g confectioners' (icing) sugar

FOR THE CARROT CAKE
Preheat the oven to 180°C - 350°F (gas mark 4). Peel the carrots and shred them in the food processor attachment fitted with a julienne disc on speed 4. Put the flour, brown sugar, baking powder, and all the spices into the bowl of the mixer flitted with the flat beater and beat on speed 1 for 1 minute. Add the eggs and oil and beat on speed 4 for 2 minutes. Lower to speed 1, add the shredded carrots, and beat for 1 minute.

Butter and flour a loaf pan and pour in the batter. Bake for 1 hour. When it is done, let cool.

FOR THE FROSTING
Put the softened butter into the bowl of the mixer fitted with the flex edge beater and beat on speed 4 for 1 minute. Immediately add the cream cheese and confectioners' (icing) sugar and beat on speed 4 for 2 minutes. Use a flat spatula to cover the carrot cake evenly with the frosting (icing).

TIP & VARIATION

To check that the cake is done, insert the tip of a knife into it. If it is done, the blade should come out clean.
You can add raisins or even chopped hazelnuts to the carrot cake.

GINGER CAKE

Serves 4–6

Preparation time: 15 minutes

Cooking time: 55 minutes

7-8 cm fresh ginger root

250 g type-45 flour

50 g brown sugar

11 g baking powder

1 tsp baking (bicarbonate of) soda

1 tbsp ginger cake spice mix

100 ml milk

250 g honey

2 eggs

Preheat the oven to 160°C - 325°F (gas mark 3). Peel the ginger and grate it finely using the Fresh Prep slicer/shredder.

In the bowl of the mixer fitted with the flex edge beater, mix the flour, brown sugar, baking powder, baking (bicarbonate of) soda, and spices on speed 2 for 1 minute.

Combine the milk and honey in a saucepan and bring to a boil. Pour into the bowl of the mixer, then add the whole eggs and grated ginger. Mix on speed 4 for 2 minutes.

Line a cake pan with parchment (baking) paper. Pour the batter into the pan and bake for about 55 minutes. When done, let cool and then remove from pan.

TIPS & VARIATION

For a stronger flavor, replace half of the flour with chestnut flour. You can also add raisins, hazelnuts, or chopped almonds. When wrapped in plastic wrap (clingfilm), this ginger cake will stay fresh for several days.

LEMON CHEESECAKE

Serves 8

Preparation time: 15 minutes

Cooking time: 1 hour

Resting time: 12 hours

100 g dry cookies (speculoos, p. 304, or shortbread, p. 76)

35 g very soft butter

600 g cream cheese

150 g crème fraîche

180 g superfine (caster) sugar

100 ml low-fat (semi-skimmed) milk

3 eggs

1 heaping tbsp type-45 flour (25 g)

1 lemon

The previous day, preheat the oven to 150°C - 300°F (gas mark 2).

Crush the cookies using a rolling pin, then put them into a large bowl. Melt the butter, pour it over the cookies, and mix. Press the cookies into the bottom of a deep 20-cm cake pan, then refrigerate while preparing the topping.

In the bowl of the mixer fitted with the wire whip, add the cream cheese, crème fraîche, and sugar, then whip on speed 2 for 2 minutes. Next, add the milk, then the eggs, one by one, whipping continuously on speed 2 until all ingredients are completely mixed. Finally, add the flour, and the lemon juice and zest. Mix for another 1 minute, then pour the mixture into the pan on top of the cookie crust.

Bake for 1 hour, then let cool in the turned-off oven until completely cool. Cover with plastic wrap (clingfilm), then refrigerate for 12 hours before serving.

TIPS

Serve this cheesecake with a fruit coulis. You can replace the lemon with 2 tbsp of vanilla extract.

FRENCH STRAWBERRY CAKE

Makes 1 20-cm cake

Preparation time: 1 hour

Cooking time: 30 minutes

Resting time: 3 hours

400 g strawberries

GENOISE CAKE

85 g type-55 flour

3 small eggs (about 150 g)

85 g superfine (caster) sugar

MOUSSELINE CREAM

350 g low-fat (semi-skimmed) milk

1/2 tsp vanilla powder

50 g superfine (caster) sugar

3 egg yolks

35 g cornstarch (cornflour)

150 g unsalted butter, softened

1 pinch salt

DECORATION AND FINISHING

20 g strawberry juice

200 g almond paste (color of your choice)

GENOISE CAKE
Sift the flour. Butter and flour a 20-cm cake ring. Preheat the oven to 190°C - 375°F (gas mark 5). Whisk the eggs with the sugar, then transfer to a double boiler (bain-marie). Heat the mixture to 50°C - 120°F, whisking constantly. Transfer to the bowl of the mixer fitted with the wire whip, then whip for 2 minutes while gradually increasing the speed. The batter should drop off the wire whip in smooth ribbons. Gently fold in the sifted flour. Set the cake ring on a baking sheet lined with parchment (baking) paper, then pour in the cake batter. Bake for about 30 minutes. Cool on a wire rack.

MOUSSELINE CREAM
Heat the milk with the vanilla powder and half of the sugar. Meanwhile, mix the egg yolks with the other half of the sugar and the cornstarch (cornflour). Once the milk reaches a boil, pour it over the egg mixture, then return to the saucepan and cook for about 3 minutes, whisking constantly. Pour into a pan lined with plastic wrap (clingfilm), folding the plastic wrap back over the surface of the cream. Refrigerate for at least 2 hours. Beat the butter to make it creamy. Put the pastry cream into the bowl of the mixer fitted with the wire whip, add the salt, and start the mixer on speed 6. Turn off the mixer, then add half the butter. Whip on speed 6 for about 1 minute 30 seconds. Add the remaining butter, then whip again for 2-3 minutes, aerating the mixture by starting on speed 6, then increasing the speed to 8.

ASSEMBLY AND DECORATION
Cut the genoise cake horizontally into thirds. Wash and hull the strawberries, then halve them from top to bottom. Line a stainless steel cake ring 20 cm across and 4.5 cm deep with a Rhodoid® acetate sheet. Set a cake disk in the bottom, then soak with strawberry juice. Next, line with strawberry halves, cut sides against the cake ring. Cover with mousseline cream. Cut the remaining strawberries into small cubes. Top the cake with a layer of strawberry cubes, then mousseline cream. Place a second disk of cake on top and soak it with the juice, then add another layer of strawberry cubes and a final layer of cream. Smooth. Refrigerate for at least 1 hour. Meanwhile, roll out the almond paste to a thickness of 2-3 mm. Cut out a 20-cm disk, then set on top of the cake.

VARIATIONS & TIPS

Use a spatula to smooth the cake perfectly. When strawberries aren't in season, you can make the same cake using pears— then it will be a pear cake. Use small pears, cutting them into neat slices 4.5 cm high to make an attractive outline. And replace the strawberry juice with pear juice. You can also use the leftover disk of cake as a tart shell, topping it with whipped cream and fresh fruit for an improvised dessert.

CHOCOLATE AND PEAR CHARLOTTE

Makes 1 18-cm charlotte

Preparation time: 1 hour

Cooking time: 30 minutes

Resting time: 1 hour

LADYFINGERS

Preheat the oven to 190°C - 375°F (gas mark 5).
In the bowl of the mixer fitted with the wire whip, whip the egg whites until they hold stiff peaks by gradually increasing the speed from 1 to 8, then set them by gradually pouring in the superfine (caster) sugar. With the mixer running, add the egg yolks and the seeds from the vanilla bean (pod). Gently fold in the flour using a rubber spatula.
Fill a pastry bag with a tip and pipe out 10-cm-long ladyfingers, one 20-cm-diameter circle, and one 15-cm circle. Sprinkle with the confectioners' (icing) sugar and bake for 10 minutes. Let cool.

CHOCOLATE BAVARIAN CREAM

Soften the gelatin in a bowl of cold water. In the bowl of the mixer fitted with the wire whip, whip the egg yolks with the sugar on speed 4 for 3 minutes. Pour the milk into a saucepan, add the chocolate in chunks, and mix to melt the chocolate. When the milk reaches a boil, gradually pour it over the egg yolks, beating constantly. Pour back into the saucepan and cook, stirring constantly, until the cream coats the back of a spoon. Next, squeeze out the gelatin and add, then let cool.
When the chocolate cream has cooled, pour the cream into the bowl of the mixer fitted with the wire whip. Whip, gradually increasing the speed from 1 to 8, until the cream holds stiff peaks. Gently combine the whipped cream and chocolate cream using a rubber spatula. Store in the refrigerator.

30° BAUME SYRUP

Pour the water into a saucepan. Add the sugar and mix well. Bring to a boil to dissolve the sugar completely, then add the pear liqueur. Let boil for a few minutes to reduce.

ASSEMBLY

Peel the pears, then cut into small cubes. Use a brush to soak the ladyfingers with the syrup. Stand the ladyfingers up around the edge of a charlotte mold. Pour in half of the chocolate Bavarian cream, add half of the pear cubes, then set the smaller ladyfinger disk on top. Add the rest of the Bavarian cream, then the rest of the pear cubes. Top with the larger ladyfinger disk. Let set in the refrigerator for at least 1 hour.
Before serving, sprinkle with chocolate shavings.

LADYFINGERS

150 g egg whites

100 g superfine (caster) sugar

80 g egg yolks

1 vanilla bean (pod), split and scraped

125 g type-45 flour

2 tbsp confectioners' (icing) sugar

CHOCOLATE BAVARIAN CREAM

5 sheets gelatin

50 g egg yolks

50 g superfine (caster) sugar

200 g milk

100 g dark chocolate

200 g cream

30° BAUME SYRUP

100 ml water

120 g superfine (caster) sugar

20 g pear liqueur

ASSEMBLY AND FINISHING

3 pears

Chocolate shavings

TIPS

For a quick version, buy ladyfingers from your local bakery, make a simple chocolate mousse (see p. 92), and use canned pears, using their syrup to soak the ladyfingers.

CHOCOLATE PRALINE
MOUSSE CAKE

Makes 1 20-cm cake

Preparation time: 1 hour

Resting time: 4 hours
15 minutes

Cooking time: 20 minutes

HAZELNUT DACQUOISE
Butter a 20-cm stainless steel cake ring. Preheat the oven to 160°C - 325°F (gas mark 3). Sift together the confectioners' (icing) sugar, hazelnut flour (ground hazelnuts), and cornstarch (cornflour). Put the egg whites into the bowl of the mixer fitted with the wire whip. Start the mixer, then gradually increase the speed to 10. Pour in the sugar until a firm meringue forms. Gently fold the sifted dry ingredients into the egg whites. Put the cake ring onto a baking sheet lined with parchment (baking) paper, pour in the batter, top with a few whole hazelnuts, then bake for about 20 minutes. Let cool on a wire rack, then remove the parchment paper.

CRUNCHY PRALINE
Melt the milk chocolate in a double boiler (bain-marie), then add the hazelnut puree. In the double boiler, stir the mixture until it is completely smooth. Crush the wafer cookies, then remove the mixture from the heat and add. Spread the mixture onto a sheet of parchment (baking) paper to make a 22-24-cm disk. Cover with a second sheet of parchment paper, then freeze flat for at least 45 minutes.

CHOCOLATE MOUSSE
In a double boiler (bain-marie), melt the chocolate, then remove from heat. Put the cream, which should be cold, into the bowl of the mixer fitted with the wire whip. Start the mixer, gradually increasing the speed to 8. Whip for about 3 minutes until the cream is just whipped. Take 3–4 tbsp of the whipped cream and mix with the melted chocolate. Once the mixture is smooth, gently fold in the rest of the whipped cream and the salt using a rubber spatula.

ASSEMBLY
Line a stainless steel cake ring 20 cm across and 4.5 cm deep with a Rhodoid® acetate strip, then with chocolate mousse. Cut an 18-cm disk out of the dacquoise and the frozen crunchy praline. Layer the cake and praline into the ring. Add chocolate mousse to fill the cake ring all the way up. Smooth the top with a spatula, then freeze for at least 3 hours.
Dust with cocoa powder and serve with caramelized hazelnuts.

HAZELNUT DACQUOISE

60 g confectioners' (icing) sugar

70 g hazelnut flour (ground hazelnuts)

15 g cornstarch (cornflour)

90 g egg whites

30 g superfine (caster) sugar

A few whole hazelnuts

CRUNCHY PRALINE

30 g milk chocolate

150 g hazelnut-cane sugar puree

75 g wafer cookies

CHOCOLATE MOUSSE

200 g dark chocolate

400 g whipping cream

1 pinch salt

FINISHING

Cocoa powder

Caramelized hazelnuts (optional)

VARIATION

For a version that is a little less sugary and 100 percent gluten-free, simply replace the wafer cookies with puffed rice. You can also add a few toasted hazelnuts to the mousse.

CAPRESE TART

Makes 1 cake for 6–8 people

Preparation time: 15 minutes

Cooking time: 30 minutes

200 g dark chocolate

100 g butter, plus 20 g for the pan

5 eggs

200 g superfine (caster) sugar

200 g almond meal (ground almonds)

1 pinch fleur de sel

Confectioners' (icing) sugar

Preheat the oven to 180°C - 350°F (gas mark 4). Butter a cake pan. Put the chocolate and butter into a bowl and melt over a bain-marie, then let cool. Separate the egg whites from the yolks.

In the bowl of the mixer fitted with the flat beater, mix the egg yolks and 100 g of the superfine (caster) sugar on speed 6 for 3 minutes. Turn down to speed 2 and add the butter and chocolate. Next, add the almond meal (ground almonds) and fleur de sel and keep beating for 1 minute. Set aside in a bowl and wash the mixer bowl.

In the bowl of the mixer fitted with the wire whip, whip the egg whites, starting on speed 1 and gradually increasing the speed to 8. Add the remaining 100 g of superfine sugar and continue whipping until stiff peaks form. Turn down to speed 2 and very gradually add the chocolate mixture. When the batter is smooth, pour it into the mold. Bake for 30 minutes, using the point of a knife to check for doneness. Let cool before unmolding and sprinkling with confectioners' (icing) sugar.

VARIATION

Replace half of the almond meal (ground almonds) with coconut flour.

VANILLA FLAN

Serves 6–8

Preparation time: 20 minutes

Cooking time: 1 hour

Resting time: 30 minutes

TART SHELL (CASE)
Mix the flour, sugar, and salt in the bowl of the mixer fitted with the flat beater on speed 1 for 30 seconds. Cut the butter into cubes, add, and mix on speed 2 for 2 minutes. Finally, add the eggs and milk, then mix until the dough just comes together. Wrap the dough in plastic wrap (clingfilm) and refrigerate for 30 minutes.

Roll out the dough on a floured work surface using a rolling pin. Butter a tart pan and line it with the rolled-out dough.

CUSTARD
Preheat the oven to 180°C - 350°F (gas mark 4).
Pour the milk, cream, and butter into a saucepan, add the vanilla, and bring to a boil.
Put the eggs and sugar into the bowl of the mixer fitted with the wire whip and mix on speed 4 for 2 minutes. Add the cornstarch (cornflour) and mix for another minute. With the mixer running on speed 2, gradually add the boiling milk. Whip for 1 minute, then return to the saucepan. Cook the cream over low heat, stirring constantly, until it thickens. Pour into the pastry shell and bake for 45 minutes.

TART SHELL (CASE)

175 g type-45 flour

20 g superfine (caster) sugar

3 g salt

90 g butter

1 egg yolk

20 g milk

CUSTARD

800 ml whole (full-fat) milk

200 ml whipping cream

25 g butter

Vanilla powder

3 eggs

150 g superfine (caster) sugar

120 g cornstarch (cornflour)

VARIATIONS
To make a chocolate version, add 100 g of melted chocolate and 1 tbsp unsweetened cocoa powder to the recipe.
For a coconut version, add 80 g unsweetened shredded coconut and replace the cream with coconut milk.

CHRISTMAS STOLLEN (ALSATIAN STOLLEN)

Serves 6–8

Preparation time: 20 minutes

Cooking time: 45 minutes

Resting time: 2 hours 45 minutes

STARTER
In the bowl of the mixer fitted with the wire whip, mix the milk, flour, and yeast on speed 4 for 2 minutes. Cover the starter with the 380 g of flour for the dough and let rise for 45 minutes in a warm place.

DOUGH
Combine all the ingredients in the bowl with the starter and flour and knead with the dough hook on speed 2 for 4 minutes. Cover with a cloth and let rise for 1 hour at room temperature.

FILLING
While the dough rises, coarsely chop the nuts, raisins, and candied (mixed) peel and soak in the rum. After the rising time is up, add the nuts, raisins, and candied peel to the dough. Dust with flour and shape into a rectangle. Roll the almond paste into a strip the same length as the short side of the rectangle. Lay it across the right-hand third of the dough. Fold the dough in half, turning it back over itself. Cover with a cloth and let rise for another 1 hour.

Preheat the oven to 170°C - 340°F (gas mark 3). Place the stollen on a baking sheet lined with parchment (baking) paper and bake for 45–50 minutes.

GLAZE
After removing it from the oven, brush the stollen with melted butter and sprinkle it with confectioners' (icing) sugar.

STARTER

50 ml whole (full-fat) milk

60 g type-45 flour

10 g compressed fresh yeast or 1 tsp active dry yeast

DOUGH

380 g type-45 flour

1 medium egg

80 g superfine (caster) sugar

150 ml whole (full-fat) milk

100 g butter, softened

1/2 tsp cinnamon

1/2 tsp vanilla powder

FILLING

50 g almonds

50 g hazelnuts

50 g raisins

100 g oz candied orange and lemon (mixed) peel

2 tbsp rum

250 g almond paste

GLAZE

30 g butter, melted

50 g confectioners' (icing) sugar

VARIATIONS

Add walnuts and candied (glacé) cherries to the filling. You can also add a little orange flower water to the dough.

COCOA PRETZELS

Makes 10 pretzels

Preparation time: 25 minutes

Cooking time: 25 minutes

Resting time: 1 hour - 1 hour 30 minutes

100 ml water

200 ml low-fat (semi-skimmed) milk

15 g fresh yeast (or 5 g dry yeast)

450 g type-45 flour

50 g unsweetened cocoa powder

30 g sugar

5 g fine salt

35 g butter, softened

50 g baking (bicarbonate of) soda

1 egg yolk

Coarse sugar

170 g dark baking chocolate

Pour the water and warm milk into the bowl of the mixer fitted with the dough hook. Add the crumbled fresh yeast and knead on speed 1 for about 2 minutes to dissolve.
Add the flour, cocoa powder, sugar, and salt and knead on speed 1. Cut the butter into pieces, add, and knead for about 5 minutes, until the butter has been completely incorporated. Increase the speed to 2 and knead for about another 5 minutes.
Cover the bowl with a cloth and let the pretzel dough rest for 1 hour–1 hour 30 minutes.

Cut the pretzel dough into ten pieces, each weighing about 85 g. Roll each piece into a rope 60–70 cm long. To shape the pretzels, form each rope into a circle. Twist the ends of the rope together twice, then bring the twisted ends toward yourself and fold down onto the bottom curve. Press lightly to fix the ends in place.

Preheat a convection oven to 200°C - 400°F (gas mark 6).
Bring the water and baking (bicarbonate of) soda to a boil in a large saucepan. Use a skimmer to blanch the pretzels for 20–30 seconds. Glaze with the beaten egg yolk. Sprinkle the bottom half of the pretzels with the coarse sugar. Bake for about 15 minutes.

Melt the chocolate over a double boiler (bain-marie). Dip the top half of the pretzels in the melted chocolate, then let stand in a cool place to harden.

CHOCOLATE
OR PLAIN
CROISSANTS

Makes 16 pastries

Preparation time: 45 minutes

Resting time: 4 hours
30 minutes

Cooking time: 13 minutes

500 g type-45 flour

10 g salt

50 g sugar

20 g compressed fresh yeast

50 g unsalted butter

1 egg

220 g milk

300 g dry butter (84% fat content)

32 sticks of chocolate for chocolate croissants

1 egg yolk for glazing

Make the yeasted puff pastry for croissants as described on p. 38.
At the end of the resting time, roll the dough out into a rectangle of about 60 x 40 cm.

TO MAKE CHOCOLATE CROISSANTS
Cut the dough into 16 small rectangles. Place 2 sticks of chocolate on each rectangle, then wrap the dough around them. Place on a baking sheet lined with parchment (baking) paper, being careful to leave space between them.

TO MAKE CROISSANTS
Cut the dough into 16 small rectangles. Fold each rectangle in half to mark the center. Score triangles into the dough (about 11 cm high and 25 cm long).
Using a large knife, trim off any extra dough with a single slice. Roll up the croissants and place on a baking sheet lined with parchment paper, making sure to leave space between them.

Let rise for about 2 hours in a warm place (25–30°C - 75–85°F).
Preheat the oven to 200°C - 400°F (gas mark 6).
Use a brush to glaze the croissants or chocolate croissants with an egg yolk.
Bake for 5 minutes, then reduce the heat to 180°C - 350°F (gas mark 4) and bake for another 8 minutes.
Let cool on a wire rack.

PISTACHIO ÉCLAIRS

Makes 10–12 éclairs

Preparation time: 45 minutes

Cooking time: 45 minutes

Resting time: 2 hours

FOR THE CRAQUELIN
Put all the ingredients into the bowl of the mixer fitted with the flat beater. Beat on speed 1 for about 2 minutes or until the dough is crumbly. Roll out the craquelin as finely as possible between two sheets of parchment (baking) paper. Freeze for 1 hour.

FOR THE PISTACHIO PASTRY CREAM
Make the pastry cream as described on p. 43, removing from heat before adding the pistachio paste, salt, and butter. Pour onto a plate and cover with plastic wrap (clingfilm) in direct contact with the cream. Refrigerate for at least 1 hour.

FOR THE CHOUX PASTRY
Make the choux pastry as described on p. 34.
Preheat the oven to 160°C – 325°F (gas mark 3) on the convection (fan-assisted) setting.
Fit a pastry (piping) bag with a 16 mm choux pastry tip (nozzle) and fill with the batter. Pipe éclairs 12–14 cm long onto a buttered baking sheet. Cut rectangles of craquelin the same size as the lines of batter and place one on top of each éclair.
Bake for about 45 minutes. Let cool on a rack.

FINISHING
Whip the pastry cream until creamy. Use a size 6 fluted pastry tip (or the tip of a knife) to make three holes in the bottom of each éclair. Fill each éclair with a generous amount of pastry cream, starting with the outer holes. Pipe the pastry cream into the middle hole until it begins to come out. Remove the excess with back of a knife.

CRAQUELIN
75 g butter

90 g sugar

100 g type-45 flour

7 g pistachio paste

PISTACHIO PASTRY CREAM
55 g superfine (caster) sugar

50 g cornstarch (cornflour)

100 g eggs (2 small eggs)

500 g low-fat (semi-skimmed) milk

1 vanilla bean (pod) or 1 tsp ground vanilla

15 g pistachio paste

1 pinch salt

1 pat (knob) of butter

CHOUX PASTRY
125 g low-fat (semi-skimmed) milk

2 g salt

2 g sugar

65 g butter

75 g type-45 flour

140–150 g eggs

VARIATION

The most popular éclairs are still the traditional chocolate and vanilla ones! To make chocolate éclairs, replace the pistachio paste with 10 g of unsweetened cocoa powder in the craquelin, and 180 g of dark baking chocolate in the pastry cream. To make vanilla éclairs, add a little vanilla to the craquelin and also to the pastry cream, perhaps even adding a splash of rum.

CINNAMON ROLLS/
KANELBULLAR

Makes 12 rolls

Preparation time: 25 minutes

Cooking time: 18 minutes

Resting time: 2 hours
45 minutes

BRIOCHE DOUGH
Make the brioche dough as described on p. 39 using the quantities listed here. After kneading, let rest 45 minutes–1 hour at room temperature; this will give the dough time to develop its flavor.

FILLING
Soften the butter. Mix until creamy. Add the sugar, salt, and cinnamon.

SHAPING
Roll out the brioche dough into a rectangle about 20 x 30 cm in size.
Spread the filling evenly over the top, leaving a 1-cm border of dough around the edge. Fold into thirds, letter-style, then use a rolling pin to roll back out into a 20 x 30-cm rectangle. Cut lengthwise into 12 strips, each about 3.3 cm wide.
Turn each strip to make a twist, then roll each twist into a roll. Glaze the rolls with the beaten egg.
Let rise in a warm place (such as a turned-off oven with a bowl of hot water) at 25–30°C - 75–85°F for about 1 hour 45 minutes. Preheat the oven to 180°C - 350°F (gas mark 4) on the convection (fan-assisted) setting. Glaze the rolls again with the beaten egg. Bake for 18 minutes. Cool on a wire rack.

BRIOCHE DOUGH

250 g fine wheat flour (or 230 g type-45 flour and 20 g wheat gluten)

25 g sugar

5 g salt

15 g fresh yeast

150 g eggs, cold

100 g butter (if possible, butter with 82% fat content)

FILLING

60 g butter

80 g brown sugar

1 pinch salt

4 tsp cinnamon

1 egg

VARIATION

You can replace the cinnamon in the filling with cardamom— Scandinavians love this kind of roll, too.

PANCAKES

Serves 4–6

Preparation time: 10 minutes

Cooking time: 10 minutes

250 g type-45 flour

30 g sugar

11 g baking powder

300 ml low-fat (semi-skimmed) milk

3 eggs

Salt

Mix the flour, sugar, baking powder, and salt in the bowl of the mixer with the flat beater on speed 2 for 1 minute. Add the milk and eggs and mix on speed 4 for 2 minutes.

Heat a skillet or frying pan with a little oil over high heat, then pour in small amounts of batter. Cook the pancakes for 5 minutes, flipping them halfway though. Repeat until all batter has been cooked.

VARIATIONS

You can add blueberries to this recipe.
To make a vegan version, replace the eggs with two bananas mashed with a fork and the milk with a non-dairy milk. For a gluten-free version, replace the wheat flour with 180 g whole-grain rice flour and 70 g cornstarch (cornflour).

JAN HAGEL COOKIES

Makes 16 (5 x 5-cm) cookies

Preparation time: 10 minutes

Cooking time: 20 minutes

150 g butter

1 pinch salt

90 g brown sugar

1 egg

200 g type-55 flour

1 tsp baking powder

1/2 tsp cinnamon

30 g confectioners' (icing) sugar

50 g slivered (flaked) almonds

Soften the butter without melting it, then put it into the bowl of the mixer fitted with the flex edge beater. Add the salt and sugar, then run the mixer on speed 1 for 1 minute. Add the egg yolk, making sure to reserve the white for the icing. Once the mixture is smooth, mix together the flour, baking powder, and cinnamon, then add to the butter mixture. Once the dough is smooth, turn off the mixer.
Butter a 20 x 20 cm baking dish, then spread the dough into the bottom using a spatula.

Preheat the oven to 180°C - 350°F (gas mark 4) on the convection (fan-assisted) setting.
Mix the egg white with the confectioners' (icing) sugar and the slivered (flaked) almonds, then spread this mixture over the cookie dough.
Bake for about 20 minutes. Serve warm.

VARIATION

For a gluten-free version, replace the wheat flour with 100 g whole-grain rice flour, 50 g cornstarch (cornflour), and 50 g almond meal (ground almonds).

RASPBERRY MACARONS

Makes 30 macarons

Preparation time: 15 minutes

Cooking time: 15 minutes

Resting time: 30 minutes

110 g almond meal (ground almonds)

110 g confectioners' (icing) sugar

110 g egg whites

120 g superfine (caster) sugar

Pink food coloring powder

Jar of raspberry jam

Sift the almond meal (ground almonds) with the confectioners' (icing) sugar into a large bowl.

Put the egg whites into the bowl of the mixer fitted with the wire whip and whip on speed 4. When they begin to form soft peaks, add the superfine (caster) sugar and increase the speed to 6. Continue whipping until the eggs have the texture of a meringue. The whites should form stiff peaks when you lift up the wire whip.

Gently fold the sifted almond mixture into the egg whites using a rubber spatula, then add the pink food coloring. The mixture should be smooth and shiny. Put it into a pastry bag fitted with a 10 or 12 mm tip, then pipe out uniform disks of about 2.5 cm in diameter on a baking sheet lined with parchment (baking) paper. Let dry at room temperature for 30 minutes.

Preheat the oven to 150°C - 300°F (gas mark 2). Bake for 12–15 minutes. After removing the shells from the oven, let cool completely before removing them from the baking sheet. Spread a spoonful of preserves over half the shells, then top with the remaining halves. Chill the macarons.

AMARETTI

3 egg whites

150 g superfine (caster) sugar

250 g almond meal (ground almonds)

2 drops bitter almond extract

Confectioners' (icing) sugar

Preheat the oven to 160°C - 325°F (gas mark 3).

Whip the egg whites in the bowl of the mixer fitted with the wire whip, starting on speed 1 and gradually increasing the speed to 8. When soft peaks form, after about 1 minute, add the sugar a little at a time. When stiff peaks form, turn to speed 2 and gradually add the almond meal (ground almonds) and bitter almond extract. Stop when the mixture is smooth.

Line a baking sheet with parchment (baking) paper. Use a spoon to make small mounds of the mixture on the baking sheet and flatten them slightly. Bake for 20 minutes. Let cool, sprinkle with confectioners' (icing) sugar, and enjoy.

V A R I A T I O N

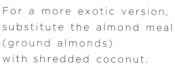

For a more exotic version, substitute the almond meal (ground almonds) with shredded coconut.

SPECULOOS

Makes 40 cookies

Preparation time: 15 minutes

Cooking time: 10 minutes

Resting time: 2 hours

175 g softened unsalted butter

175 g brown sugar

250 g type-45 flour

1 tsp baking powder

1 tbsp cinnamon

1/2 tsp ground ginger

1 pinch salt

1 egg

Mix the butter and brown sugar in the bowl of the mixer fitted with the flat beater on speed 2 for 2 minutes. Add the flour, baking powder, spices, and salt and mix on speed 2 for 1 minute. Add the egg and mix on speed 4 for 1 minute. Gather the dough into a ball, flatten, and wrap in plastic wrap (clingfilm). Refrigerate for 2 hours.

Preheat the oven to 160°C - 325°F (gas mark 3). Roll out the dough on a floured work surface using a rolling pin, and cut out the cookies with a cookie cutter. Place the cookies on a baking sheet lined with parchment (baking) paper, spaced apart, because they will spreading during baking. Bake for 10 minutes. The speculoos will be soft when removed from the oven but will harden as they cool. Repeat with the remaining dough.

VARIATION & TIP

You can replace half the cinnamon with a quatre-épices spice blend and add the finely grated zest of one orange. To decorate your speculoos with homemade icing, mix some confectioners' (icing) sugar with a little lemon juice and decorate using a cone or pastry bag.

FLOATING ISLANDS

Serves 4-6

Preparation time: 10 minutes

Cooking time: 5 minutes

CUSTARD SAUCE (POURING CUSTARD)

6 egg yolks

100 g sugar

500 ml low-fat (semi-skimmed) milk

2 tsp praline paste

MERINGUE

6 egg whites

80 g sugar

TOPPING

2 tbsp praline powder

CUSTARD SAUCE (POURING CUSTARD)
Make the custard as described on p. 42.

MERINGUE
Preheat the oven to 180°C - 350°F (gas mark 4).
In the bowl of the mixer fitted with the wire whip, whip the egg whites, gradually increasing the speed from 1 to 8. When they begin to hold soft peaks, add the sugar a little at a time. When the whites are well whipped, pour them into a cake pan and bake for 3 minutes. Let cool.

TOPPING
Pour the custard sauce (pouring custard) into soup plates or bowls, then add 1–2 tbsp of meringue. Sprinkle with praline and serve cold.

TIP

You can sprinkle the meringue with cocoa powder, caramel, slivered almonds, etc.

COOKIE ICE CREAM

Serves 6

Preparation time: 10 minutes

Cooking time: 15 minutes

Resting time: 1 hour 20 minutes

6 cookies (see p. 90)

400 ml low-fat (semi-skimmed) milk

1 tbsp vanilla extract

6 egg yolks

150 g sugar

100 g Mascarpone cheese

Pour the milk into a saucepan, add the vanilla extract, and bring to a boil.

Meanwhile, put the egg yolks and sugar into the bowl of the mixer fitted with the wire whip and whip on speed 4 for 3 minutes, until the mixture becomes pale. With the mixer running, gradually add the boiling milk. Pour the mixture back into the saucepan and cook over low heat, stirring constantly with a wooden spoon, until it begins to thicken. Once the cream coats the back of the spoon, remove the saucepan from the heat.

Wash the bowl of the mixer. Put the Mascarpone cheese into the bowl and whip on speed 4 for 2 minutes. Gradually pour in the hot cream and whip for another 2 minutes. Let cool for 1 hour.

Once cool, start the ice cream maker on speed 2 and pour in the mixture. Churn the ice cream for 20 minutes. Once the ice cream is set, add the crumbled cookies and churn for another few minutes. Store in the freezer.

TIP

You can replace the cookies with speculoos, Rheims pink biscuits, or even shortbread.

BERRY SORBET

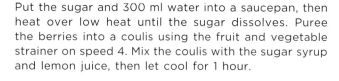

Serves 6

Preparation time: 10 minutes

Cooking time: 5 minutes

Resting time: 1 hour
20 minutes

450 g berries (strawberries, raspberries, blackberries)

200 g sugar

Juice of 1/2 lemon

Put the sugar and 300 ml water into a saucepan, then heat over low heat until the sugar dissolves. Puree the berries into a coulis using the fruit and vegetable strainer on speed 4. Mix the coulis with the sugar syrup and lemon juice, then let cool for 1 hour.

Once cool, start the ice cream maker on speed 2 and pour in the mixture. Churn the sorbet for 20 minutes. Transfer to a container and keep in the freezer until ready to serve.

VARIATION & TIP

For a gourmet version, replace the sugar syrup with 200 ml crème fraîche. You can add some pieces of fruit or even candy once the sorbet is set, letting it churn for another 1 minute. You can use frozen berries for this recipe.

ALMOND MILK
APRICOT
ICE CREAM

Serves 4

Preparation time: 20 minutes

Cooking time: 20 minutes

Resting time: 1 hour 20 minutes

8 apricots

20 g butter

30 g brown sugar

1 tsp vanilla powder

3 egg yolks

100 g superfine (caster) sugar

500 ml almond milk

Wash the apricots and cut them into small dice. Brown the butter and apricots in a skillet or frying pan for 5 minutes. Next, add the brown sugar and vanilla and let caramelize for 5 minutes. Remove the pan from heat and set aside.

In the bowl of the mixer fitted with the wire whip, mix the egg yolks and sugar on speed 4 for 2 minutes. Meanwhile, pour the almond milk into a saucepan and bring it to a boil. With the mixer running, gradually pour the boiling almond milk over the egg yolks. Pour the mixture back into the saucepan and cook, stirring constantly, until it thickens slightly like a light (pouring) custard. The cream should coat the back of a spoon. Pour it into a large bowl and let cool for 1 hour.

Once the mixture is completely cooled, start the ice cream maker on speed 2 and pour in the mixture. Churn for 20 minutes. Once the ice cream has set, add the diced apricots and churn for another few minutes. Store in the freezer.

VARIATIONS & TIPS

This ice cream can be made with peaches or nectarines. You can also replace the almond milk with rice or hazelnut milk. To accentuate the almond flavor, you can add a few drops of bitter almond extract. Just before serving, sprinkle the ice cream with toasted sliced (flaked) almonds.

CARAMEL
ICE CREAM

Serves 4

Preparation time: 30 minutes

Cooking time: 5 minutes

Resting time: 1 hour
20 minutes

**380 g caramel
(dulce de leche)**

**150 ml low-fat
(semi-skimmed) milk**

400 ml whipping cream

3 eggs

Pour the caramel, milk, and cream into a saucepan. Heat, stirring, to melt the caramel.

Meanwhile, separate the egg whites from the yolks. Whip the yolks in the bowl of the mixer fitted with the wire whip on speed 4 for 2 minutes. With the mixer running, gradually pour in the caramel mixture. Pour the mixture back into the saucepan, then cook over low heat, stirring with a wooden spoon. The cream should thicken like a light (pouring) custard. Check if the cream is cooked by running your finger over the cream-covered spoon; it should leave a clear trail. Pour into a large bowl and let cool for 1 hour.

Wash the mixer bowl, then pour in the egg whites. Use the wire whip to whip them until they form stiff peaks, raising the speed gradually from 1 to 8. Gently fold in the caramel cream using a rubber spatula.

Start the ice cream maker on speed 2 and pour in the mixture. Churn the ice cream for 20 minutes. Remove from the ice cream maker and keep in the freezer until ready to serve.

T I P

You can make the caramel yourself (see p. 256) or buy it prepared from a store.

FROZEN YOGURT

Serves 4

Preparation time: 25 minutes

Resting time: 20 minutes

800 g Greek-style yogurt

100 g confectioners' (icing) sugar

1 tsp vanilla extract

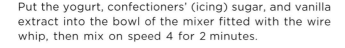

Put the yogurt, confectioners' (icing) sugar, and vanilla extract into the bowl of the mixer fitted with the wire whip, then mix on speed 4 for 2 minutes.

Start the ice cream maker on speed 2 and pour in the mixture. Churn for 20 minutes. Remove from the ice cream maker.

Serve the frozen yogurt with a fruit coulis, chocolate chips, pieces of fruit, crunchy cereals, crumbled cookies, crushed candies, etc.

VARIATIONS

Blend 300 g strawberries and add the resulting pulp to the frozen yogurt. You can also make this recipe with reduced-fat yogurt.

HONEY NUT NOUGAT ICE CREAM

Serves 6–8

Preparation time: 30 minutes

Cooking time: 10 minutes

Resting time: 12 hours

CARAMELIZED NUTS

75 g whole almonds

75 g hazelnuts

50 g honey

50 g sugar

NOUGAT ICE CREAM

3 eggs

100 g sugar

100 g honey

400 ml whipping cream

CARAMELIZED NUTS

Preheat the oven to 180°C - 350°F (gas mark 4). Spread the almonds and hazelnuts on a baking sheet lined with parchment (baking) paper and roast them in the oven for about 5 minutes.

Caramelize the honey and sugar in a small saucepan. When the caramel is a dark gold, add the roasted nuts, mix, and pour onto a sheet of parchment paper. Let cool, then coarsely chop with a knife.

NOUGAT ICE CREAM

Separate the egg whites from the yolks. In the bowl of the mixer fitted with the wire whip, whip the egg yolks with the sugar on speed 4 for 3 minutes. Pour into a bowl and set aside.

Wash the bowl, then use it to whip the egg whites to stiff peaks using the wire whip, gradually increasing the speed from 1 to 8.

In a small saucepan, bring the honey to a boil, then pour it in a thin stream over the beaten egg whites while running the mixer continuously on speed 4. Add the egg yolk and sugar mixture. Set aside in a large bowl.

Wash the mixer bowl, then pour in the cream, which should be very cold. Whip the cream using the wire whip, gradually increasing the speed from 1 to 8. Gently fold the whipped cream into the egg mixture. Add the caramelized nuts and mix gently.

Pour the mixture into a large cake pan covered with plastic wrap (clingfilm). Freeze for at least 12 hours before serving.

VARIATION & TIP

Try different nuts and dried fruits: pistachios, raisins, pine nuts, etc.
Serve with a caramel sauce (see p. 262) or a berry coulis (see p. 322).

PANNA COTTA
WITH MANGO COULIS

Serves 4

Preparation time: 10 minutes

Cooking time: 20 minutes

Resting time: 2 hours

PANNA COTTA

1/2 sheet gelatin (3 g)

1 vanilla bean (pod)

800 ml whole (full-fat) milk

300 ml whipping cream

25 g sugar

MANGO COULIS

**450 g mangoes
(fresh or frozen)**

25 g superfine (caster) sugar

PANNA COTTA
Immerse the sheets of gelatin in a bowl of cold water. Split the vanilla bean (pod) and scrape out the seeds. Pour the milk, cream, and sugar into a saucepan, then bring to a boil. Remove from the heat. Squeeze the excess water from the gelatin and add to the saucepan. Pour into 4 glasses or ramekins. Cover with plastic wrap (clingfilm) and let set in the refrigerator for at least 2 hours.

MANGO COULIS
Meanwhile, peel the mangoes, then puree into a coulis using the fruit and vegetable strainer on speed 4. Pour the coulis into a saucepan, add the sugar, then cook over low heat for 15 minutes. Let cool.

Before serving, pour the mango coulis over each panna cotta.

TIPS & VARIATION

You can replace the mango coulis with a coulis made from berries, peaches, apricots, etc. Be sure to modify the amount of sugar in the coulis according to the acidity of the chosen fruit.
For a vegan version, replace the milk and cream with coconut milk and the gelatin with 1 g agar.

BERRY TIRAMISU

Serves 6

Preparation time: 20 minutes

Cooking time: 5 minutes

450 g berries

70 g sugar

2 eggs

250 g Mascarpone cheese

12 ladyfingers (see p. 278)

Make the berry coulis: Puree 300 g of the berries using the fruit and vegetable strainer on speed 4. Pour into a saucepan, add 20 g sugar, and bring to a boil. Let cool.

Separate the egg whites from the yolks. In the bowl of the mixer fitted with the wire whip, mix the egg yolks with 25 g sugar on speed 4 for 3 minutes. Add the Mascarpone cheese and continue to whip for 2 minutes. Transfer to a large bowl and set aside.

Put the egg whites into the bowl of the mixer and whip, gradually increasing the speed from 1 to 8. When they begin to hold soft peaks, add the remaining 25 g sugar, a little at a time. Once the whites are firm, use a spatula to fold them into the Mascarpone mix.

Quickly dip the ladyfingers into the berry coulis.
Place a layer of whole berries into the bottom of a glass, cover with cream, then cut a ladyfinger in half and add. Add another layer of cream, ladyfingers, coulis, and fresh fruit, topping with a final layer of cream. Repeat with the five remaining glasses. Serve cold.

VARIATION & TIP

You can replace the ladyfingers with Rheims pink biscuits.
You can also flavor the cream with rosewater.

HAZELNUT
SPREAD

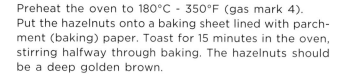

Makes 2 jars

Preparation time: 10 minutes

Cooking time: 10 minutes

200 g hazelnuts

150 ml whipping cream

100 g dark chocolate

100 g milk chocolate

40 g confectioners' (icing) sugar

2 tbsp neutral oil (peanut or grapeseed)

1 tsp vanilla extract

Preheat the oven to 180°C - 350°F (gas mark 4). Put the hazelnuts onto a baking sheet lined with parchment (baking) paper. Toast for 15 minutes in the oven, stirring halfway through baking. The hazelnuts should be a deep golden brown.

After removing from the oven, puree them using the food grinder fitted with the fine plate on speed 4. Run the resulting puree through the food grinder again to make sure the hazelnuts have released all their oil.

Heat the cream in a saucepan. Add the dark chocolate and milk chocolate, both broken into pieces, let stand for 3 minutes, then mix until smooth.

Place the hazelnut puree in the bowl of the mixer fitted with the flex edge beater. Add the cream and melted chocolate, confectioner's (icing) sugar, oil, and vanilla extract. Mix on speed 4 for 2 minutes. Transfer the mixture to two jars and seal securely. Keep in the refrigerator and eat within 15 days.

TIP & VARIANTION

You can add a pinch of fleur de sel.
Use any nuts you like: Almonds, cashew nuts, macadamia nuts, etc.
You can replace the neutral oil with coconut oil.

APPENDICES

CONVERSIONS TABLE

MAXIMUM BOWL CAPACITY

3.3 L

- 680 g all-purpose (plain) flour
- 8 egg whites (medium)
- 1.8 kg cake batter
- 2 kg mashed potatoes
- 60 cookies

4.8 L

- 1 kg all-purpose (plain) flour and 800 g whole-wheat (wholemeal) flour
- 12 egg whites (medium)
- 1 L whipped cream
- 2.7 kg cake batter
- 2 kg bread dough (stiff yeasted dough)
- 3.2 kg mashed potatoes
- 108 cookies

6.9 L

- 2.2 kg all-purpose (plain) flour and 1.75 kg whole-wheat (wholemeal) flour
- 19 egg whites (medium)
- 1.9 L whipped cream
- 4.5 kg cake batter
- 3.8 kg bread dough (stiff yeasted dough)
- 3.6 kg mashed potatoes
- 168 cookies

INGREDIENTS

	US	EU		US	EU
			Brown sugar	1 cup	130 g
Crème fraîche	1 cup	240 g	**White sugar**	1 cup	130 g
Country-style cream	1 cup	240 g	**Nib sugar**	1 cup	200 g
Light cream	1 cup	240 g	**Pearl sugar**	1 cup	150 g

VOLUME

US		EU
1 cup	16 tablespoons	240 ml
1/2 cup	8 tablespoons	120 ml
1/3 cup	5 tbsp + 1 tsp	80 ml
1/4 cup	4 tablespoons	60 ml
1 tablespoon	3 teaspoons	15 ml
1 teaspoon		5 ml
1 fluid ounce		30 ml
1 US quart	4 cups	~1 L

TEMPERATURE

F°	C°	Gas mark (FR)
400	205	6
350	175	4
300	150	2
250	120	1/2

WEIGHT

US		EU
1 ounce		28 g
1 pound	16 ounces	454 g

LENGTH

US		EU
1 inch		2.54 cm
1 foot	12 inches	30 cm

Milk	1 cup	240 ml		
Butter	1/2 cup	113 g	1 stick	4 ounces
Butter	1 tablespoon	14 g		
Oil	1 cup	200 g		

Fine salt	1 teaspoon	5 g
Flour, white or whole-wheat	1 cup	125 g

conversions
table

TABLE
OF CONTENTS

table of contents

INDEX
BY RECIPE TYPE

333

index by
recipe
type

INDEX
BY ATTACHMENT

index by
attachment

INDEX BY INGREDIENT

index by ingredient

ACKNOWLEDGEMENTS

To all the Passionate Makers who have inspired us since 1919.

KitchenAid Europa, Inc. Nijverheidslaan 3, box 5, 1853 Strombeek-Bever, Belgium
https://www.kitchenaid.eu/

COLLECTION DIRECTOR
Alain Ducasse

DIRECTOR
Aurore Charoy

EDITORIAL MANAGER
Alice Gouget

EDITORS
Fanny Morgensztern and Jessica Rostain

PHOTOGRAPHY
© Rina Nurra

FOOD STYLING AND PLATING
Ayumi Iida

PHOTOENGRAVING
Nord Compo

Printed in Spain by Ingoprint on paper from responsibly managed forests.

ISBN: 978-2-84123-967-2
Legal deposit 3rd quarter 2018

© Ducasse Édition 2018
Ducasse Édition
2, rue Paul-Vaillant-Couturier
92532 Levallois-Perret Cedex